WHAT EVER HAPPENED TO BABY JAMES?

WHAT EVER HAPPENED TO BABY JAMES?

A true story of abduction, secrecy, betrayal, and discovery by a Victim of Georgia Tann and the Tennessee Children's Home Society

DON W. BOEHNER

To order additional copies of this book, contact:
Xlibris LLC
1-888-795-4274
www.Xlibris.com
Orders@Xlibris.com
612169

CONTENTS

DEDICATION

Lucretia Martin Boehner
My Friend, My Wife, My Lover, and My Editor-In-Chief
~
The Bowman Families and Relations
The Griffith Family and Relations
Evelyn Deakins and the Harris Family
Jeffi White and Family
Les R. Morris
Marion County Historical Society
The Van Hoosier Family, and,
To the thousands of children victimized by the TCHS

COMING HOME

Here's from a family
Lost but now found
Here's to your journey
Now home you are bound
Here's to a history
Of life you've not seen
A puzzle piece missing
Of things that have been
Here's to your searching
And traveling roads
The weight of your mind
And millions of loads
Here's to the questions
Where answers were few
We are your family
And we welcome you
JEFFI WHITE
September 18, 2011
. . . o0O0o . . .

The above poem was written by my Cousin Jeffi of Griffith Creek, Tennessee, for our reunion with my birth families September 18, 2011. It very accurately portrays the warm and loving receptions we received on our first visit to the area in which I was born, from both the Arnold Lafayette Griffith and Flossie Louise Bowman families.

PROLOGUE

"Hello . . . Hello? Is this Ms. Hall?" Mary Hawkins-Wright asked impatiently due to endless problems with the new phone lines. "Hello, yes this is Margaret Hall". "Hi Margaret . . . Mary up in Jasper." "Yes Dear. Sorry I missed you on my visit to Dunlap last week." "Oh, that's alright; been very busy this May . . . must have been some queer shine in the hills nine months ago", Mary laughed quietly to herself with a rare display of humor. "But I want to tell you . . . a woman came in to the Clinic on the 5ᵗʰ, we've seen her before; the name is Bowman. She gave birth this morning to a premature boy; slightly over three pounds and going to take some care for a month or more." "What is your assessment?" Margaret asked with an excitedly high-pitched enthusiasm. "The mother is Hill Trash you know, worked at a bar in Sequachie . . . has a record here with Marion County Welfare; is now living with her sister in Whitwell. She has no husband . . ." "Oh is that so", Margaret declared in her thick Tennessee drawl. "What does it look like Mary?" "Well minus the pounds, a blue-eyed, blonde-haired baby boy." "Is it marketable?" "It will put on weight over the next month or so; should be ready by August", Mary coldly calculated. "Fine; I'll let Ms. Tann know". Margaret paused pending her next question. "Have you talked to the mother yet?" "No, not yet; I planned to do that early this afternoon while she's still a little groggy." "That's probably for the best . . . don't want her too upset when she makes the surrender". Margaret agreed and added, "I'll send you the cover letter next week to get the process started; do what you can to secure it before the end of next week." "My dear Margaret, you are just an angel in disguise; just what would these poor urchins do without you", Mary cooed with absolute adoration. "My dear, what would we do without them . . . why we would be working in Sequachie"! The pair broke into

---

a spontaneous fit of laughter. "Don't worry Margaret, I'll take care of
everything, there should not be a problem, Mary assured. Goodbye."

The above telephone call is not real, I just made it up. But the story line surrounding this possible call between Mary Hawkins-Wright and Margaret Hall is all too real. It is a call that was probably made dozens of times in 1949 between the Tennessee Children's Home Society in Chattanooga, and Wright's Clinic in Jasper, Tennessee. Letters between these agencies from May 1949 through December 1949, contained in my adoption files, demonstrate the collusion and communication between them, solely for the purpose of identifying my birth, selection for adoption with or without my birth parents' permission, and abduction pending falsified adoption to out-of-state adoptive parents.

I was born James Arnold Bowman in Marion County, Jasper, Tennessee, in a two-story white-framed house locally designated as Wright's Clinic, and later Wright's Hospital, located on the north end of Jasper on Highway 41.

To my best knowledge, a Dr. McMillian delivered me on May 8, 1949, although the date is somewhat suspicious as is my Certificate of Live Birth #141-49-28302. The document executed in handwriting on plain typing paper, failed to reflect a time of  birth, the signature of the delivering physician, a Father's name, and was not witnessed/officiated until June 13, 1949. My adoption would not be 'officially' completed until 1953. The Tennessee Children's Home Society (TCHS) operated by Georgia Tann had a nasty habit of altering birth dates, parents' names, and other information to conceal adoptees' and parents true identities. I believe the date was made up, selected because of its easy-to-remember historic significance, VE Day, the end of WWII, four years earlier. The entire Live Birth Certificate, including witness signature, is all the same handwriting, which speculates possibly neither Dr. McMillian, or the officiating witness, Steve Bryar, wrote the certificate. A second 'official' birth certificate #141-49-25202 issued by the State of TN on June 8, 1949, already reflected my adoptive name as Donald Walter Boehner, and the names of my adoptive parents; strangely living at an address in Fullerton, California, they would not live at until mid-1953. The only correspondences which survived destruction, between the TCHS and my adoptive parents, were September 30, 1949 and January 15, 1950.

At our Bowman Family reunion in September 2011, not long after we arrived, I was met by Cousins Hazel Van Hoosier Kilgore and Glenda Van Hoosier Walden, daughters of my Mothers' sister, Josephine (Josie) Bowman Van Hoosier Glenda exclaimed, "My God boy, we thought you were dead." Both could hardly believe I had really survived and were truly remorseful they did not know I had been stolen and taken away. The unsolicited story I received was that my mother Flossie had been told I died at Wright's Clinic and they would take care of the remains for her. Flossie had no reason to doubt their story as she had taken me back into Wright's Clinic several months after I was born with an acute stomach ailment. It was all the excuse the TCHS needed. In conspiracy with Marion County Social Welfare, the TCHS removed me from Wright's Clinic in the middle of the night, as was their standard operating procedure, concealing me at the Chattanooga orphanage of the TCHS until December 8, 1949, when I was then secreted to Georgia Tann's orphanage home in Memphis, Tennessee. During those previous four months, Tann and her loyal associates conspired to create a plausible history, fabricate required background and birth documents, and prepared for the required Surrender form.

I first received my Tennessee adoption records on May 6, 2009, two days before my 60th birthday. Phone conversations with Children's Services explained that Tann had ordered the destruction of all TCHS files, but not all were burned, and some files only partially destroyed. I first noticed the lack of 'introductory' documents or paperwork, or correspondence which evidenced how my adoptive parents came in contact with the TCHS. Careful review of the file left me with more questions than answers. Due to Georgia's preference being white male infants, blonde hair, blue eyes and outwardly healthy, I was selected by a Spotter for TCHS as "highly adoptable". I was picked, marketed, and sold like so much meat, as were so many other Tennessee children, some being marked for death and disposal in the nearby Memphis swamps, with others facing fates worse than death working in labor camps, or simply institutionalized. Some have survived to demand justice for all. I am one of those survivors; consider this scenario:

'The black Buick Special lumbered through the empty main street of Jasper, the sound of its engine muffled in the dense, humid air of a 3a.m. August morning. It sways right as it turns onto an unmarked dirt road, then an immediate sway to the left into the rear driveway of a dimly lit home on Highway 41. The driver bounces the car to a sudden stop simultaneously ordering his female companion from the car. "You must hurry . . . hurry, we don't have much time; the Constable will be making his rounds soon . . . and don't slam the door!" She softly closed the car door behind her and trotted up to the rear of the Clinic to be startled by an awaiting nurse behind the screen. "Are you here for it?' the voice asked sternly. "Yes Ma'am." "It's about time, been no end to its crying." The screen door sprang open and a white bundle plunged onto her chest. "Good bye". The nurse disappeared with no further word. The aide returned to the car and entered the rear seat. "Is it alive or dead?" the driver asked routinely. "Alive, but drugged with liquor", was the response. "Then we go back to Chattanooga". The sedan pulled from the driveway and invisibly slipped through town and onto Highway 24, returning to the Chattanooga children's home with their commodity'.
1.

I was gone, quickly and silently, secreted over a 3-4 month period to Chattanooga, then to Memphis, then to Nashville, and finally by train in the company of Tann's Assistant Alma Walton, to be delivered to my adoptive parents, Walter and Sidonia Boehner, in Los Angeles, California, in January 1950. My adoptive parents were charged $5,000.00 for my adoption. I would not know any details about my natural parents until 2008.

No one ever asked, "What ever happened to Baby James?"

In preparations and considerations for this book, I first consumed prior writings by Barbara Bisantz Raymond ("*The Baby Thief*") and internet resources from *Wikipedia* in 2009-2010, followed by books written by Dr. John Standridge ("*The Delaney Kids—Bought & Paid For*"), Linda Tollett Austin ("*Babies For Sale*"), and, the website *www.tennesseechildren.tripod. com* in 2011-2013. Through the excellent literary works of these authors, the transition of adoption practices, introduction of the Tennessee Children's Home Society, and corruption at the hand and direction of Georgia Tann, are expertly documented. I sincerely thank the individual authors for their passion and heartfelt desire to bring this tragic history to light, and an understanding as to what may have happened to me in 1949. I did not have the desire or the means in which to prepare an exhausting expose' rehashing events and applicable legal precedence in the Society's chain of events, I did find however prior writings did focus on that particular aspect. Dr.

Standridge's book focused more so upon the individual adoptions of he and his siblings, and I found it very interesting of his inclusion of some of the forms and correspondence involved in the adoptions, which are very similar to mine. Interestingly, I found that Dr. Standridge and I were infants under the charge of Georgia Tann in Memphis at the same time in late 1949—early 1950.

In January 2013, I began drafting my ideas for a book on my adoption. I decided to include not only my physical adoption in 1949, but to carry the story into how my entire life was affected by the fact of my adoption and not being "blood relation". I do not desire to write the grand expose' of my Boehner family or create the impression of a 'pity party'. I had a wonderful life growing up, with loving parents however misguided in desiring to keep my adoption secret and family members who will always be close to my heart. It has been difficult to recall let alone write about these matters for all to see, as by nature, I am a very private person. Outside of my son, daughter, and Uncle Vern, the Boehner family is not aware that I have found my biological family. So armed with these new thoughts and ideas, I have attempted to comprise my documented history of the good and bad, supported by actual adoption case documents, letters, court papers, and my best recollections of my past.

The following chapters will escort the reader from my abduction from Wright's Clinic in Jasper, through secret incarceration in Chattanooga, Memphis, and Nashville, tracing the individual steps taken by Social Welfare, Judge Camille Kelly, and the Tennessee Children's Home Society in creating a legal adoption out of thin air, and my life as an Adoptee.

This is my story.

CHAPTER 1

Tennessee Children's Home Society

The organization existed under the direction and laws of the State of Tennessee, sometime before Beulah George "Georgia" Tann's arrival from Mississippi at age 25. Tann found an atmosphere in Memphis in which she could thrive. Judges, state officials, social workers, doctors, nurses, lawyers, court clerks, and local officials most likely to be associated with the protection of her endeavors and law enforcement who would be most likely charged with any investigation concerning questioned adoptions, gathered on Tann's payroll. The TCHS's  power reached out of Tennessee to place its own favorable adoption representatives in New York, Georgia, Alabama, Florida, and Southern California as primary destinations. By the late-1930's, Georgia Tann was entrenched and in charge of Tennessee adoptions. The TCHS increased adoptions from an average of 5-10 per month, to over 200 per month and climbing. No one of authority ever asked the proper interrogatives; everyone knew the answers.

Tann knew the adoption laws of Tennessee as her work in the field created a majority of policy and procedure throughout the United States. What was not written is where did all these new adoptions come from? Who cared? By 1945, the TCHS recorded 300-400 children died while under Tann's care due to gastrointestinal disease, starvation, abuse and neglect in a four-month period; and that is the reported deaths. More children disappeared into the swamps bordering Tennessee and Mississippi and very few investigations were launched let alone successful. The Society operated with complete immunity until 1949, and through that time is responsible for an estimated 5,000 illegal adoptions of stolen children. The money was flowing for Georgia Tann and for her employees and associates. The fabrication mill for laundering falsified adoptions was in full swing, from "Spotters" such as Ms. Mary Hawkins Wright who operated Wright's Clinic in Jasper, TN, actually acting primarily as an unwed mother's birthing clinic for the TCHS, to Ms. Margaret Hall, Field Supervisor for the Chattanooga branch of the TCHS. I believe my delivering physician Dr. McMillian obviously knew the difference from delivering babies at his office down the street from the clinic, which he routinely performed, and the circumstances of children born at Wright's Clinic. My handwritten Certificate of Live Birth #141-49-28302 *(Fig. 1)* evidences the lack of detail from a normal birth affidavit, leading to a prior knowledge that additional information was not necessary in these cases.

Shelby County Juvenile Court Judge Camille McGee Kelley assisted in the legal formation of my adoption and performing the investigation into the legal assignment of who my Father would (Fig. 34) be. Neither candidate for fatherhood would ever be contacted regarding my adoption. Lenard Arnold Harris was easily accessible in 1949, living in Tracy City, Tennessee, where Flossie said he was living. Arnold Lafayette Griffith was in the US Army

Guardhouse at Fort Jackson, South Carolina and very easily contacted through his Commanding Officer or the Provost Marshal's Office. Judge Kelley reported to Tann, as noted in a typewritten 'History Sheet' (Fig. 2) from December 8, 1949, by the TCHS, that no dissolution of marriage existed between the divorce Flossie stated she retained an attorney for, and the Order where Flossie was told by Judge Kelley she could remarry, was simply and conveniently made to disappear to expedite my adoption. It was not until 2012 that I discovered a link associating the TCHS and the Law Firm of Hooper & Miller, Los Angeles, California, (*www. children.tripod.com*) as being the law firm who handled the California portion of my adoption proceeding as filed in the Superior Court of California, County of Orange, Santa Ana, California, court case number A-22307 *(Fig. 3)*. In all case files presented for this court and case, none maintained any origination dates, signatures, or file court stamps affixed. Court searches in

2009, 2012, and 2014 for this case number and file was not found of record in Orange County. It is apparent my adoption was never recorded in California, and never existed outside of the Los Angeles law firm.

The first correspondence occurring between Flossie Bowman and the Tennessee Children's Home Society is dated May 16, 1949, by Miss Margaret Hall, Field Secretary, *(Fig. 4)* in part:

> *"A few days ago when I happened to be visiting at Wright's Clinic in Jasper, Miss Wright mentioned to me that you might be interested in adoptive services for your baby. She was not sure just what arrangement you planned to make for it when it is ready to leave the hospital . . ."*

Flossie received the typewritten letter and responded on May 20, 1949 *(Fig. 5)*, in her own handwriting:

> *"Dear Friend*
>
> *I am not interested in giving my baby away and I didn't say I was going to give it away. I have a home for both of them with me. Some people was trying to get me to give the baby away.*
>
> *I wouldn't give one of my children away for nothing in the world. That was someone else's idea not mine. Thank you for offering to help me but I don't need that kind of help.*
>
> *Signed: Miss Bowman"*

On May 25, 1949, Miss Mary Hawkins Wright of 'Wright's Hospital' received a report from Miss Hall regarding Flossie's response *(Fig. 6)*, and stating in part:

> *". . . You have no doubt heard from her yourself by now. She is probably one of those persons who look upon adoption as "sinful . . .*
>
> *Signed: Margaret Hall"*

I wish to make a special note regarding these letters. The Reader will notice in Hall's letter above she refers to the baby as "it". This coldly demonstrates children were just chattel for a profit to these disgusting individuals.

According to file notes within my adoption packet, I was born approximately 2 months premature. I was brought home by Flossie to her sister Josephine's residence in Whitwell, TN, within a month or so after birth. By early September 1949, I had been returned to the Clinic for health concerns and treatment of gastrointestinal problems in retaining food. It would be the last time my Mother would see me in her lifetime. Flossie Louise Bowman Little passed away in Whitwell, Tennessee, on July 26, 1993, without ever knowing I survived.

During the first few months of my existence, the TCHS and their Field Secretary with collusion from Mary Hawkins Wright were hard at work documenting Flossie's personal history. Their work was represented in the 'Case History' *(Fig. 7)* not presented until the date of December 8, 1949, and involved information from Flossie's Marion County Welfare file. There they received information from Flossie's assistance application, and information on Flossie's Father, Joseph William Bowman receiving public assistance prior to his death in 1946. This detailed information would have been sufficient to 'create' the initial adoption interview normally necessary to establish the foundation for adoption proceedings.

The specific date in which Flossie was notified of my death, and in what manner, is unknown. Surviving relatives close to Flossie believe it was around late August, early September 1949, when the Clinic called with the news. Georgia Tann had already known for some time of my existence and marketability for adoption, as documented by my Tennessee birth certificate #141-49-85202 dated June 8, 1949 *(Fig. 8)*, showing my adoptive name and parents. Once I was stolen and secured in Chattanooga, Tann wasted no time in contacting my adoptive parents with the good news in a personal letter dated September 30, 1949 *(Fig. 9)*, as follows:

> *"Mr. and Mrs. Walter A. Boehner 505 South Sunset Blvd., Temple City, California*
>
> *My Dear Mr. and Mrs. Boehner:*
>
> *This letter is written to advise you that your home has definitely been accepted for the placement of a child.*
>
> *You will doubtless recall that Mrs.(Alma) Walton explained to you that due to many applications already on file and approved, it may be from six months to a year after the home had been verified and approved before a placement could be made. However, in some instances we are*

able to make a placement much sooner than we had expected and you may rest assured that just as soon as the proper child is available, we will get in touch with you.

Due to congested traveling conditions, it is my advice that you have one of our trained workers bring the child to you. Traveling, at best, is difficult, even for a trained worker, and this suggestion is made for this reason.

Sincerely yours,
SIGNED: Georgia Tann Assistant State Superintendent
TENNESSEE CHILDREN'S HOME SOCIETY".

By this point in time, Georgia Tann was growing weaker from cancer and the organization's day-to-day functions were slowly being absorbed by trusted assistants and workers in Memphis and Nashville. State and federal investigators responding to ever-increasing reports and complaints of Tann's illegal adoption scheme began to appear on the doorsteps of TCHS locations around the state, weakly probing and summarily dismissing most assignments. Georgia could see the handwriting on the wall. She instructed her staffs around the state to begin pulling all adoption files and burn them, beginning with adoptive parent and birth parent information specifically. It also became clear that the remaining illegal children in her charge had to be dealt with . . . and dealt with quickly. As any shrewd retailer would do, Tann assessed her current inventory, assigned categories for dissemination of the product, and distributed for profit. Infants and children ravaged by physical, sexual and mental abuse in Georgia's care were primarily killed or sent directly to mental institutions where the procedure of "Lobotomy" was widely practiced. Older children deemed "unadoptable" were shipped to labor camps, work farms, or sold into servitude under some of the cruelest of circumstances. What little care and attention offered, was utilized to promote the adoptable children; those children were worth a lot of money.

By the end of October 1949, I had been held in secrecy for a month or more and the TCHS was getting a clear picture that my illegitimate adoption could continue as no inquiries had been made after my untimely demise. Miss Margaret Hall drafted an alleged letter to Flossie dated October 24, 1949 *(Fig. 10)*, stating in part:

"I understand that you are interested in our service and would like to discuss plans for your baby. Can you come to my office in Chattanooga? You see it is a matter of signing papers which I believe can be done more confidentiality here, or perhaps in Jasper. If you cannot come here, could you take the baby to Miss Wright and meet me there sometime . . ."

All that was left was the creation of propriety, the illusion of thoroughness, and a signed adoption surrender form; I don't believe Miss Hall's letter of the 24th ever left her office.

CHAPTER 2

A Legal Adoption

"Oh, what a tangled web we weave when first
we practice to deceive".

Edgar Allen Poe

By the end of October 1949, my official adoption birth certificate *(Fig. 8)* had allegedly been in print since June 8, 1949. My adoptive parents had already been selected as potential parents by Georgia Tann, possibly even prior to my birth *(Fig. 9)*. It was now time for the Tennessee Children's Home Society to craft my circumstances to fit the requests of the client. In my adoption package is a "Request For a New Certificate of Birth By Adoption" *(Fig. 11)*, executed on September 12, 1952, displaying my adoptive parents' names, and their address of 500 El Camino Drive, Fullerton, California. The 'official certificate dated 1949 was not prepared until 1952 and receipt of this request. My adoptive Father was of German/Scottish decent, and my adoptive Mother of German/French lineage. Both were devout Lutherans. In a questionnaire interview sheet, this information would have been provided to the TCHS during the application process; as was income, investments, property holdings, insurance benefits, membership organizations and pension/retirement benefits. They also would have been asked during their application process as to their preferences concerning an adopted child. This presented the roadmap in designing my case study reports insuring what my adoptive parents requested was exactly what they received. Between September and December 1949, two separate case history reports *(Fig. 2) (Fig. 7)* were made of record by the TCHS, both correlating my adoptive parents' wishes in my adoptee's background. It seems Georgia had found the 'perfect' match for Mr. and Mrs. Boehner. Both histories contained contradictory information, not even being able to provide the same description of Flossie Bowman, of whom they allegedly had repeated contact with. But most importantly, a trail of paper had to be created leading to the successful surrender of the baby for adoption. It is my opinion that task fell upon Mary Hawkins Wright and Miss Margaret Hall between October 31st and December 7th, 1949.

The following letter handwritten in pencil is reportedly from Flossie Bowman and alleged in response to Miss Margaret Hall's letter of October 24, 1949 *(Fig. 10)*. This letter was not written by Flossie; penmanship, grammar, spelling does not match Flossie's original letter of May 20, 1949. The letter in question is as follows *(Fig. 12)*, to wit:

> *"Whitwell, Tenn October 31, 1949*
> *Miss Margaret Hall*
>
> *Dear Ms. Hall*
>
> *In answer to your letter received in regards to the baby, I can meet you in Jasper at Mrs. Wright's on Nov the 15th at one o'clock. So let me know if you can be there at that time.*
>
> *Yours Truly*
> *Flossie Bowman"*

The TCHS in Chattanooga was quick to allegedly respond on November 3, 1949, with another typed letter from Miss Hall *(Fig. 13)*, in part:

> ". . . I have received your letter this morning. I will meet you at Miss Wright's on November 15, 1949, at 1:00 P.M. Thank you very much.
>
> Yours very truly,
> (Miss) Margaret Hall
> Field Secretary"

The letters contained in my adoption file continued in an alleged back-and-forth communications between Hall and Flossie; December 2, 1949 *(Fig. 14)*, and December 7, 1949 *(Fig. 15)* leading to December 8, 1949, and the forgery of my surrender to adopt form *(Fig. 16)*. It is plain and simple that Flossie Bowman did not sign the surrender document *(Fig. 17)* on her child, and obviously not present or aware of such proceeding. On the surrender form, Arnold Lafayette Griffith (misspelled as Griffeth) was listed as my Father. No relinquishment for adoption was ever sought or received from either Griffith or from Harris. Not one of the dozens of family members living in Whitwell and Griffith Creek were ever contacted concerning my birth or the alternative to adoption.

Letters and signatures alleged from Flossie Bowman, after May 20, 1949, are forgeries including the December 1, 1949 letter. In the "Child's Own Family" case history of December 26, 1949 *(Fig. 18)*, Margaret Hall states, in part, ". . . *she (Flossie) replied that she was not interested in releasing her child for adoption (the letter was not written in the mother's handwriting we later learned)*". Miss Hall or someone realized the writings and signatures would not pass inspection, so she/they discounted Flossie's original letter containing the refusal of services rendering as useless, and establishing the remaining forgeries as legitimate. The letter could not be used as contradictory evidence against the TCHS.

Between December 8th and December 9th, 1949, I was secreted to Memphis and placed in Georgia Tann's custody, evidenced by the

Examinations and Recommendations Record *(Fig. 19)* executed between December 9th and December 13th. The medical record documented that on December 13, 1949, I was turned over to the care of Mrs. (Alma) Walton at 8:30p.m. I recall only one other reference to Walton where Tann indicated in the 'acceptance' letter of September 30th that my adoptive parents had spoken to her. I have the impression that Mrs. Walton was the 'Adoption Coordinator', handling initial inquiries for adopting parents, and also, staging children leaving for various destinations including Nashville, Tennessee. No other records survived documenting my time in Memphis, or exactly when I was secreted to the Nashville Chapter of the Tennessee Children's Home Society, or transported by train to Southern California.

Although I was now permanently out of sight, I was still much in the minds of Georgia Tann, Mary Hawkins Wright, and Margaret Hall. The atmosphere for Tann's operation was becoming more difficult, and scrutiny much more defined as 'outsiders' became more involved in adoptive activities. It did not however affect Georgia's experienced conspirators from continuing to cover their tracks, and adoptee's backgrounds. To illustrate the point, I have included in part a letter dated December 12, 1949, from Miss Margaret Hall, TCHS Field Supervisor, to Miss Mamie Lou Hall, (Marion) County Director, Department of Public Welfare, Jasper, Tennessee *(Fig. 20)*, to wit:

"Dear Miss Hall:

I was very sorry I missed seeing you when I was in Jasper on December 8th. I wanted to tell you that the above named child (James Arnold Bowman) had been released to the Tennessee Children's Home Society for the purpose of adoption.

The mother was interested in placing this child for adoption at the time he was born. You no doubt know that he was born prematurely and required considerable attention. It seems that members of her own family urged her to keep the child." . . . *"Finally, on November 18th, we accepted custody of the child for a period of study and observation to determine adoptability and on December 8th arrangements for release were completed."* . . . *"It was not however, until after we obtained final release that we learned this child had been included in an AFDC grant. We felt sure you would like to have this information."* . . . *"The mother stated that she, too, would get in touch with you."* . . . *"We wonder if your record contains verification of the mother's divorce from Lenord Harris . . ."*

The above letter is a contrived synopsis, intended to support the fairytale history they developed and perpetuated. I do not know if the two Halls represented above are related or not. Being familiar with Flossie's meager financial condition, I find it difficult Flossie would willingly give up an easy half of her welfare grant, as she was already receiving a grant for my sister, Linda Jane Griffith, born in 1947. Surrendering me for adoption would get her nothing, and was against her moral judgment and desire pursuant to her letter of May 20, 1949, to the TCHS. After working as an investigator and independent civil/family law paralegal for 31 years, I know how people can just change their mind, but Flossie was motivated by three things in 1949, money, alcohol, and family; probably about in that order of preference;

Flossie was only 20 years old in 1949 with a reported 6th grade education. Any adoption would have been, at least, mentioned to her sister Josie Bowman Van Hoosier, whom she lived with at the time of my birth, or one of her brothers living in the immediate area. Neither the Bowman, Griffith nor Harris families would have tolerated an adoption if known or suspected. It is what I saw in their faces of the Bowman's and Griffith's at our reunions in 2011, remorse, embarrassment, shock, and ultimate disbelief that such a horrible tragedy could happen within their own family . . . and no one knew.

On September 9, 2012, I found my Lenard Arnold Harris family through Evelyn Coppinger Deakins, the Niece of Lenard Harris. Evelyn described her Uncle as a nice man who loved children, and a fondness for drinking and gambling. She stated he lived in Tracy City, Tennessee all of his life until moving to Murfreesboro, Tennessee, just before his death. She told me that Lenard never new of me, and if he had been contacted, would not have allowed the adoption to occur. With Evelyn's information and description of Mr. Harris as being 5'6, dark brown hair and brown eyes, it placed Lenard out of the running for Fatherhood, at least mine anyway. I am 6'0, light brown hair, and blue eyes with similar facial features of my biological Mother.

As I page through my adoption file which I keep in a three-ring binder on my desk, the next recorded event is the "Record of Placement" *(Fig. 21)*, loosely dated December 14, 1949. It gave me pause when I noticed the "Number of Record" being 7702; predictably I being the 7,702nd child victimized. A very strange and ill-prepared form in that two different typewriters were used to enter, and correct wrong information; the listed address of *"500 El Camino Drive, Fullerton, California"*, would not be our home for another 4 years, as noted in a letter dated February 26, 1952, from Mrs. Natalia L. Tschekaloff, Adoption Worker, Department of Social Welfare, State of California *(Fig. 22)*. The letter stated, in part:

> *"The family have recently purchased a new home at 500 El Camino Drive, Fullerton, and they are moving to this home in the near future. They are planning to sell their current home".*

I say loosely dated as "Dec." and "1949" are typed, the day is handwritten in. This form was not prepared in 1949, or 1950, or 1951. I also submit that my "Certificate of Live Birth" *(Fig. 8)* prepared by the State of Tennessee allegedly on June 8, 1949, Line number 5D reflects my adoptive parent's address as *"Fullerton"*. This certificate was faked no earlier than late 1952.

My birth Mother refused to name my Father when I was born, although I believe that Arnold Griffith's name was brought into the inquiry through

Flossie's earlier AFDC Grant for my sister Linda. Mr. Griffith was listed as Linda's Father in December 1947, a year and five months before my birth. The issue of establishing a "legal Father" became of major concern and the topic of numerous correspondences between the Marion County Department of Public Welfare; the Tennessee State Department of Public Welfare, Nashville; the Department of Social Welfare, State of California; and the TCHS. In a letter dated December 22, 1949, Mamie Lou Hall, Marion County Director of Department of Public Welfare *(Fig. 23)* wrote, in part:

> ". . . *Flossie was of the opinion that she was divorced from her husband (Lenard Arnold Harris), but according to the Circuit Court Clerk of Marion County, this divorce has not been granted.*"

In contrast and contradiction, I offer a letter dated May 13, 1952, from Miss Doris June Vinton, Child Welfare Worker, Marion County Public Welfare, to Vallie S. Miller, Director, Division of Field Service Consultants, Department of Public Welfare, Nashville *(Fig. 24)*, in part as follows:

> ". . . *We have still been unable to find any verification of the divorce of Miss Bowman from Mr. Harris either in Circuit Court records or Chancery Court records. It would seem if Mr. Harris has gotten the divorce from Flossie Bowman that she was still married to him at the time of the birth of the child*".

> ". . . *Mrs. Griffith was also certain that she got a divorce from Leonard Harris as she remembers the judge telling her that she could get married again and she insisted that the judge was Judge (Camille) Kelley. Judge Kelley's circuit included Tracy City*".

In the above correspondence from December 22, 1949, an admission from the Marion County Circuit Court Clerk, states covertly a divorce was apparently filed, just not completed. In an earlier report, Judge Kelley told the TCHS she was unable to find a divorce of record in Marion County. There are certain facts to know regarding law and procedure upon this issue. It is true today as it was in 1949, that a married person cannot legally marry another without divorce from the latter. As a paralegal, I understand a fine line may exist from a dissolution being 'started' and not 'completed' by the filing of the final case documents; I've prepared hundreds of default and contested judgments on which final actions had been delayed for any number of reasons, and over period of years. If Flossie had retained a lawyer, to which the name of a Mr. McClarney was introduced as someone Flossie saw, but allegedly did not follow through, initial documents which Flossie did file would still be of record in the civil/family law case index of the court. That is of course unless the case was removed from court records . . . simply made to disappear. Considering such possibility and the known involvement of Judge Kelley in establishing the legality of illegal adoptions it would have been an 'easy fix' for this problem. In the true nature and procedure of the TCHS to hide birth parent(s) and children to deter and prevent unwanted disclosure or discovery of illegal activities, I believe Flossie's divorce was eliminated from existence with the help of Judge Kelley. With Harris as the designated Father, any claims or inquiries would fall on innocent ears as he would have no clue about any adoption or my existence. Griffith was never identified outside of Department of Public Welfare and TCHS internal documents. This paved the way to complete the illegal adoption without a separate surrender signed by the Father as they allegedly could not find them. They could now use the fabricated surrender form of December 8th as the sole basis to complete my sale.

During the time I was being hidden and processed for adoption, Georgia Tann and her affiliates in State Legislature and local politics were cashing in on immense political influences to change existing adoption laws to their favor. New laws sanctified "confidential birth certificates" eliminating searchable methods of identifying ones birth parents; adoption records became sealed, confidential property of the State of Tennessee; and in 1950 committed one of the most despicable crimes against the stolen children of Tennessee – decreeing that all adoptions handled by the Tennessee Children's Home Society, are legal. These laws and other self-enacted policies were designed to discourage, hinder, derail, deem unlawful, and/or prevent the ultimate indictment of anyone associated with a TCHS adoption. No one was ever held accountable to those 7,702 children for the violation of their Civil Rights, the felonious criminal acts committed against them, torts too numerous to mention, and to most the priceless loss of the parent or child due to time, not knowing the true story of the other before their death.

Our records were sealed until 2006 when finally opened under the Freedom of Information Act. It took me a year and several attempts in 2009 and 2010 to gain copies and the original child photographs from the surviving welfare and TCHS records; I estimate approximately a third of my TCHS file had been destroyed consisting primarily of all preliminary adoption applications, correspondence, and file notations regarding the introduction of my adoptive parents to the Tennessee Children's Home Society.

A very interesting letter was written July 12, 1951, from J.O. McMahan, Commissioner, Tennessee Department of Public Welfare in Nashville *(Fig. 25)*, going to my adoptive parents living in Temple City, California. The form letter presents the first acknowledgment that a problem existed, that the TCHS was *"reorganized"* and a weak admission stating in part,

> . . . *"This has been due to many complexities arising from the disregard of both Tennessee and California laws in the extensive inter-state placement of children by the Shelby County Branch of the Tennessee Children's Home Society which, as you know, is now closed and enjoined by court order from further operations".*

I have included the full photocopy of this letter *(Fig. 25)* in the photo section of the book. To coin a phrase, I'll bet that letter freaked my parents out, to the max!

Georgia Tann died of cancer on September 15, 1950, followed by burial in Hickory, Mississippi. She deserves no more postscript than that.

The TCHS orphanage home in Memphis was closed December 15, 1950; 8 months before the above letter was written by McMahan. He further issues instruction concerning restricted contact by my adoptive parents to the TCHS, and personal assurance of propriety *(Fig. 25)*, to wit:

> *"Any communications concerning children whose adoptions have not been legally consummated should be directed to this Department, attention Mrs. Vallie S. Miller, Supervisor of Adoptions".*

> *". . . we wanted you to know that the necessary steps are being taken to insure the legality of adoptions pending with the view of giving security to all the parties concerned".*

On July 26, 1951, Vallie S. Miller, Supervisor of Child Welfare, TCHS, Nashville, took full advantage of the recently passed law regarding birth certificates of their adoptees, executing my "Application For Confidential Verification of Birth" *(Fig. 26)*, requesting a certified photostatic copy "for purposes of adoption". Of course my certificate had been altered, showing falsely it was prepared in 1949. No one noticed, or cared the certificate was null and void.

On September 12, 1952, the Juvenile Court of Davidson County, Tennessee at Nashville, case number 103-605, *TCHS v. Leonard A. Harris and Flossie Louise Bowman* *(Fig. 27)*, entered the Final Decree for the Tennessee portion of my adoption, as recorded in Minute Book 101. The grounds for my adoption were "neglect" and "abandonment". Process service of the Petition documents was performed by publication; I assume most likely in a Nashville paper where no family member would possibly see it. The legal process overseen by Judge D.F. Blackmon was a sham, a whitewash, in part to hurry and get rid of this black cloud of adoptions hanging over Tennessee. I had already been with my adoptive family in California for three years and nine months.

Now that Tann was gone, it was left to the minions to face the ramifications left in her wake, and clean up the pending adoptions by whatever means necessary. In my case, the TCHS was still plagued by two issues; supplying a "Certification of Relinquishment" *(Fig. 28)* form documenting no claim by a biological father; and, no case files of a divorce by Flossie from Lenard Harris. The relinquishment form was executed on September 15, 1952, pursuant to *Tennessee Public Acts of 1949 and 1951*. I was released for adoption solely based upon the fraudulent Surrender document of December 8, 1949 *(Fig. 16)*, and the false case history *(Fig. 18)* created by the Marion County Public Welfare, Mary Higgins Wright of Wright's Clinic, and Miss Margaret Hall, TCHS.

CHAPTER 3

The California Connection

There is no paperwork or correspondence in my adoption file identifying the Law Firm of Hooper and Miller, Suite 1101-1104, William Fox Building, 608 South Hill Street, Los Angeles 14, California, outside of the Order For Adoption *(Fig. 29)* allegedly filed in Orange County, Santa Ana, California. When and how Hooper & Miller, Esquires, received the assignment is undocumented. The stated hearing and Order For Adoption came on March 4, 1953, case number A-22307. An official search for these records in 2011, by case number failed to locate any filing of record. It possibly could be the fault of an unenthused worker dispatched to the dungeon of antiquity on a smoke break, or, something a little more serious.

The question of 'How did the Boehner's find out about the TCHS to seek an adoption?' is still somewhat of a mystery. As related earlier, no preliminary documents survived destruction by Tann's employees in Memphis and Nashville. The facts are widely known of various famous movie stars using Georgia Tann for numerous adoptions, how did they find out about a Tennessee adoption agency?

FRIENDLY GREETINGS...

from the
TENNESSEE CHILDREN'S HOME SOCIETY
SHELBY COUNTY DIVISION
MEMPHIS, TENNESSEE

I believe the answer is simple . . . advertising. With the amount of money charged by Tann for out-of-state adoptions, she could afford repetitive ads in the Los Angeles Times, New York Times, and other metro papers within her target states. Tann developed advertising art depicting happy children, sad children, happy parents . . . anything which would pull at the readers' heart, and pocketbook. No local addresses were used in these ads, all referring to the TCHS, Shelby County, Memphis, Tennessee. Everything went through Georgia Tann . . . everything!

Because of the address listed on the law firm letterhead, being six blocks from downtown L.A., the firm had been very successful for some time to afford a suite of offices in that locale. I would estimate their billable rate per hour was in the mid-hundreds in 1953; equal to thousands of dollars per hour at today's rates. The Partners' offices would have been mini-mansions equipped with over-stuffed leather chairs, original paintings, a bar, and the always-present portrait of Abraham Lincoln. They would have displayed the latest in modern inventions, such as the Dictaphone and switchboard circuitry for multi-line telephones. They would have greeted visiting clients while seated behind an enormous oak desk, framed by lavish drapes with a view over the Los Angeles skyline, the desk usually adorned with a green glass & brass Bankers lamp, and the Scales of Justice; always an important piece to advertise honesty when you are a lawyer. A family portrait usually adorned a discreet corner of the office to display the appearance of 'caring for the little people'. The attorney would be prepared with papers neatly placed to one side and would know his script and exactly what to say including 'chit-chat', and exactly how long the meeting would take. This law firm was

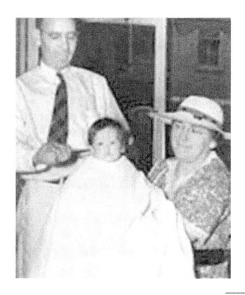

not the type of firm to see 'regular' adopting parents off the street. If you were Joan Crawford, Alan Ladd, June Allyson, or even Smiley Burnette who also adopted through the TCHS, that would most likely occur, but sadly not with Mr. and Mrs. Boehner of Temple City.

Assignments and orders to Hooper & Miller came straight from Georgia Tann as all newspaper advertisements for adoptive children around the country referred directly to Georgia Tann, TCHS in Memphis as the only contact. Having been Tann's conspirator in California for some time, the firm knew exactly what they needed in forms and procedure to seek a 'legal' adoption order in California. A telephone call and a package in the mail from Tann containing their 'fee' would take care of the matter, very quickly and easily as every form involved in a California adoption . . . could have been accomplished in their office without ever involving the Court system.

As a former California licensed Private Investigator and independent paralegal, I have had the misfortune of seeing attorneys go bad to the point of falsifying filings, signatures, casework, and process service results. In 1953, a majority of court file stamps were small hand-rotating rubber stamps where the date was manually adjusted. The 'By' signature line for the Deputy Clerk was a separate rubber and ink hand stamp, placed at the same time as the file stamp, documenting the item was received by the Court. Even in 1953, the Clerk's Office in Santa Ana would have been a beehive of activity dawn to dusk. I have personally had cases where the Clerk's Office was so busy, they handed me the court stamps and asked if I would conform the originals and copies for them; I happily did so, minus the signatures of course, escaping possibly an hour or more waiting in line. With the dishonest history of Hooper & Miller receiving essentially bribe money to launder stolen children adoptions in Southern California, I would like to share my conjecture of educated possibilities of what may have transpired:

I surmise that once I was selected as adoptable, the fabrication mill was set in motion to prepare the required documents from initial contact through sanction of a Tennessee adoption. Upon an Adoption Order issued in Tennessee, Hooper & Miller were notified by Tann to prepare for another adoption to be filed in California. Tann compiled the Tennessee court and relative TCHS paperwork, and their check, sending by air mail to Los Angeles. On receipt, it would be delivered to the lawyer addressed on the envelope unopened. He would review the contents, and would already have one secretary or paralegal performing the actual forgery of the adoption filings. No one else in the offices would notice as outwardly it would be observed as just another adoption on just another day. After close of business, the legal assistant would retrieve the official court stamps from their hiding place and quickly conforms the original and copies. The assistant had sometime before stolen the stamp sets from the Clerk's Office which was hardly noticed; they come up missing all the time. A quick example of a Deputy Clerks' signature, and a Judge's signature, is snatched from a nearby file and she duplicates the required signatures perfectly . . . lots of practice. She places the completed work in a file folder and stores inside her

locked desk until the next day where she proudly displays her work to
the attorney. "Good work Tricksie . . . bet you have a bonus at the end
of the week", he says with a smile and a pat on the rear. The attorney
removes the original documents and hands the assistant back the copies
to distribute as normal; the originals he slips into his leather valet case
and taken home, the papers to be burned later to start the BBQ.

Whether a pleading or an order, it is highly plausible my California adoption was prepared, filed, and ordered in this manner, without ever seeing the inside of a Court office. There is no evidence the California Superior Court of Orange County was ever in contact with the California Department of Social Welfare concerning any request for filed copies directly. All case documents were funneled from the TCHS, to Hooper & Miller, to Social Welfare, or, between the TCHS and Social Welfare directly. The Court, in normal circumstances, would only deal with Hooper & Miller directly. The California Department of Social Welfare relied solely on what was provided to them without question, regardless of their prior knowledge of falsified adoptions from Tennessee. Again, a state power in charge of the welfare of human lives failed to ask, "What ever happened to Baby James?"

By February 16, 1953, J.O McMahan was replaced as Commissioner, Tennessee Department of Public Welfare, with Mrs. Christine C. Reynolds who had a lot of catching up to do with ongoing adoptions. It was brought to the attention of Ralph L. Goff, Area Director, Department of Social Welfare, Los Angeles 12, California *(Fig. 30)*, in a letter of the same date, stating in part:

"We are making a monthly review of the adoptions still pending of
children in the guardianship of the Tennessee Children's Home Society
and find that on October 2, 1952, we transmitted to your office the
necessary documents for the consummation of the above adoption (James
Arnold Bowman)." ". . . would appreciate a report from you concerning
its status and, if the final decree has been granted, we would appreciate
your communicating with the attorney (George A. Hooper of Hooper
& Miller) relative to providing us with a certified copy of the decree
and forwarding the documents necessary for securing a new birth
certificate".

Within sixteen days from the date this inquiry was written, an alleged hearing was held on March 4, 1953, in Santa Ana, California, to finalize my California adoption. Attended only by George A. Hooper representing my adoptive parents, the process of my adoption was completed and an Order of Decree *(Fig. 29)* issued. In a follow-up letter dated March 20, 1953, from

Helen Chandler, an Adoptions Worker for the California Department of Social Welfare, to Commissioner Reynolds in Nashville *(Fig. 31)*, to wit:

> *"We are enclosing a certified copy of the order of adoption granted by the Superior Court of the State of California, in and for the County of Orange, in the above captioned matter. This order was granted on March 4, 1953. The attorney for Mr. and Mrs. Boehner, Mr. George A. Hooper, is taking responsibility for sending the documents for the issuance of a new birth certificate.*

> *Our department is now closing its files and considers this matter completed".*

The deception was complete. Once the State of Tennessee sanctioned my abandonment and placed me under the 'legal' charge of the Tennessee Children's Home Society pursuant to the suit filed on my adoption in Nashville, the remainder of the process in California was solely a rubber stamp upon the tainted, falsified work of the TCHS.

Tennessee swept most of us under the rug of shame as new state legislators, case workers, and federal social workers became increasingly familiar with Georgia Tann's operation and wide-spread corruption. The State of Tennessee's response and unwritten rule, was to, 'get it over with and never speak of the TCHS adoptions again . . . ever.' The state rushed through pending TCHS adoptions, designated the files confidential state property, and sealed all files. They believed the issues and problems were now behind them, the unfortunate children forgotten, and the officials went on to live their lives unaffected by the tragedy they eagerly created. Again, no one was held accountable.

I was safe now, free from the organization who removed me from my biological family, safe with my parents living the high life in 1953 Southern California. Every afternoon was filled with Roy Rogers, The Lone Ranger, Lash LaRue. Howdy Doody, the Mickey Mouse Club, and, our yearly fishing trip to Lake George. But even with the adoption finalized, my adoptive parents were very worried. They knew there was a problem with my adoption and the TCHS, probably not to the extent as actually existed, but enough for both to decide they would keep my adoption a secret, and requested my Uncles and Aunts to do the same. I was not to find out any details of my adoption until after both had passed away; but in 1957, their deception was exposed when a Cousin told me I was adopted. It began decades of stories, lies, and betrayal, continuing to February 2010 and the passing of my mother Sidonia who took her information to the grave rather than tell me the story of my adoption.

CHAPTER 4

BETRAYAL

My parents were loving, doting people who wanted only the very best for me. Birthdays and Christmas' were always special and I was definitely spoiled rotten. I was brought up strictly in the Lutheran Church doctrine and rounded up each Sunday to attend church and Sunday school. We moved to Fullerton for a short time, then on to La Habra Heights and the avocado ranch my Father had purchased in 1953. My Grandmother Boehner and my Uncle Vernon lived at the bottom of Lamat Road next to the gravel drive going back to my parents' home. Uncle Ed and Aunt Mary also lived in a small apartment up from the main house. One of my best memories is coming home from elementary school and stopping at Grandma's for a boiled hot dog. In about 1954-55, my Uncle Fred and Aunt Sally Krohe, my Mother's sister, purchased some grape acreage located in Tulare County outside of Exeter, California. We made a number of trips to visit our family, and my parents finally made the decision to sell the avocado ranch and purchase 20 acres of oranges and lemons, owned at that time by the John

Curl, Sr. family. It was just before our move to Exeter I was told I was adopted. I was 7 years old.

My Cousin, eleven years old at the time, and I were playing one evening in her room. I have never asked her what prompted her to tell me, "Your mom and dad are not really your mom and dad." I protested they were and she insisted they were not. As our protests became louder, Aunt Sally stepped into the doorway and said matter-of-factly, "She's right Donnie; they're not your mom and dad". My Mother was in the adjacent kitchen, heard Sally's declaration, and in absolute horror charged into the bedroom yanking me by the arm into the adjacent, dark living room. There she was forced to admit that I was adopted. Sidonia explained that I was born in Tennessee and that my real Mother could not afford me, and had to give me away. She told me they loved me very much and would keep me forever. I didn't understand; they were still the same parents I had just fifteen minutes ago; they loved me; I didn't really care about the rest of it. It was quite a while before their relationship with the Krohe's warmed and I was again allowed to play with my Cousin. The secret was out and I had no idea how this disclosure would affect my relationship with my adoptive parents through my adulthood. My Cousin's telling me of my adoption was not an act of betrayal, only an eleven year old repeating what she heard the grown-ups say.

My aunt, uncle and cousin were always good to me and I always looked forward to seeing them as I grew up. Aunt Sally did have sort of a queer sense of right and wrong when it came to my adoption and how I came to be. In one story, she told me I was left lying on a table as an infant, abandoned by my mother in a house where someone heard me crying, and took me to the orphanage. I was about 10 at the time. In another story, Sally told me I had been left in a mailbox for the Postman to find. I was 14 and graduating from 8th Grade at Sequoia Union Elementary at the time of that story. I don't believe my relatives knew the truth of my adoption; possibly not even knowing the history or problems with the TCHS. They could even be stories which my mother told to fortify, or justify the adoption. The affect was that I did not know the truth. I was told repeatedly my birth mother did not want me and gave me away. To this day I have no cause as to why Sally would tell a kid such tales, for what means, or for what purpose. It was no secret how most of the relatives thought, following the death of my father in 1983; I was adopted, not blood relation as my cousin Joan loudly proclaimed, "He's not entitled to anything!"

The turning point of my true affections, I believe after later consideration, is when my Mother started using the fact of my adoption as punishment to alter my behavior. I was not an unruly child but became more self-governing which mostly did not see eye-to-eye with my Mother's control of things. My acting out and behavior problems were mainly dealt with by room restriction or a paddle; but as I became older and too big for the paddle, Mom resorted to more psychological warfare to combat my increasing defiance. *"If you're not happy here, we can certainly call the orphanage and have you sent back"*, became a familiar phrase, as did, *"If you don't love us anymore, we'll send you back to your mother who didn't want you in the first place"*. It would be the 'carrot & stick" approach used to affect my behavior. In retrospect, it didn't work. My Father, never used the threat of return to correct my attitude, in fact, never mentioned the Tennessee Children's Home Society or my adoption to me during his lifetime. He did however mention how 'stupid' I was in most circumstances. His favorite saying to me was, *"It is better to let people think you're stupid, than to open your mouth and remove all doubt"*. It is a saying that has stuck with me to this day. My Father was intimidating to most who met him, 6'5, 240 pounds, and an I.Q. to match. In Orange High School, Orange, California in the mid 1930's, Dad was given an I.Q. test and rated at 187 percentile. He was offered a partial scholarship to the Massachusetts Institute of Technology, but his family was unable to afford the tuition. While I struggled as a Freshman in high school studying Algebra, Dad had an occasion to apply for an advanced Technical Engineer position with Pacific Telephone & Telegraph in Visalia, California. While I had no interest to figure out why x=z, Dad had purchased a book entitled, "Physics". He sat in his recliner scribbling on pads of paper, while watching the evening news, and taught himself Physics, in about 3 months of part-time study. My lack of interest in my education absolutely fueled my Father's disappointment and frustration in my attitude. He would become so frustrated he would grab me by the hair and slam my head onto the arm of the sofa repeatedly. But the more they threatened, the more stubborn I became; I also stopped communicating all thoughts and feelings, wants or ideas, in fear of being stupid, once again. I became withdrawn, refused to participate in class discussions and was terrified if I would be called on for an answer to anything. Mom continued using her threats of 'deportation' until I entered college in 1967. But a promise I made as a child some eight years before, would take its place, and used as a replacement 'stick' until 2005.

My parents had apparently had an argument, serious enough to the point my Mother was considering leaving, or having to leave. She was sitting in their bedroom on the edge of the bed crying and called me in. She gave me a hug and asked, *"If I leave your Father, do you love me enough to come with me? You love me don't you?"* Of course I said yes. *"Will you always take care of me?"* Again, I said yes. At 10 years old I had no idea how that moment would alter my life. In turn, my parents seemed to replace family love and joy with money; if I was good, I got 'things', if I was bad I was sent out to work on the ranch and threatened with being returned if I was not happy. It eventually had no effect and I drifted unmotivated through high school, managing to graduate in a college preparatory course of study in 1967. As was expected of

me, I enrolled at the College of the Sequoias (COS) in Visalia, California, with Political Science as my major, and Psychology as my minor. I primarily viewed my time at COS as an extension of my social calendar and completely uninterested in my course of study. By November 1968, I had amassed approximately fourteen speeding tickets, had my license suspended for thirty days, and was threatened with jail time on my last offense. Judge Del Rey of the Pixley Justice Court said it straight and to the point, ". . . either go to jail or join the military, your choice". I had already learned my draft number was up, so it was a choice I knew was forthcoming, just not

so soon. On December 28, 1968, I was sworn into the U.S. Army and on my way to Fort Lewis, Washington for basic training. Dad was pleased on the opportunity I would grow up, but Mom was horrified that I would do such a thing, considering my enlistment as a personal affront against her. In actuality, the kid who left in 1968 would never return, and a person who they would never understand, returned in his place. I eventually served with the 1/69th Armor as a Scout under the 4th Infantry Division at Camp Radcliffe, An Khe, South Vietnam, being awarded the Purple Heart and Bronze Star. After Vietnam, in 1970 I applied and was accepted into Military Intelligence and attended the Counterintelligence Special Agent Course at Fort Huachuca, Arizona. I became a field Special Agent assigned to the Resident Office in Lincoln, Nebraska. I left military service in April 1973, returning to California to establish my law enforcement career. When I was released in 1969 from the burn ward at a military hospital in Japan and returned home my Mother asked me, "Did you kill anyone?" I paused to answer knowing how the truth would affect her. "Yes I did". She never forgave me for telling her the truth.

In 1970, my Grandmother Bertha Labahn passed away in Anaheim, California. I was recently returned from Vietnam after being wounded in combat, and had been assigned to the 75th Rangers, Ft. Hood, Texas, and unable to attend her funeral. It was during this time I first heard from my Mother that I was not a "blood relative and therefore not entitled to any inheritance". Sidonia told me that following Grandmother Labahn's death,

Fred and Sally Krohe broke into the garage containing my Grandmother's furniture and effects, removing items of value as they desired, followed by claims they did not possess anything. Mom claimed she personally saw a number of these items boldly displayed in the Krohe's home and the homes of my Cousin, warning me that they would try to take her antiques and collectibles rightfully mine. I received no proof of Mom's claims, but she continued with this warning through 2004.

The true extent of my family's dislike for my lack of heritage surfaced in March 1983 following my Father's burial in Exeter Cemetery during the reception at our ranch in Exeter. I remember I was sitting at the kitchen table surrounded with my close friends from high school, my wife at the time, and my cousin. From the adjacent living room I began to hear loud talk between my Uncle Al and Aunt Leona, Aunt Sally Krohe, and my Cousin Joan Moiola. As I started listening, I heard they were arguing about whether I was entitled to an inheritance since I was not a blood relative. My Mother protested that my adoption made no difference and I was as much a Boehner as if she had given birth to me. Sally pointed out it did make a difference and related to my Cousin LaVonne Boehner Chastain whom had been adopted by my Uncle Edgar Boehner after marriage to my Aunt Betty; the point being LaVonne was not blood relation either and should not be entitled to inheritance. Joan loudly backed Sally's interpretation which in turn Uncle Ed told her she didn't know what she was talking about. That comment drove Joan into a rage letting loose with a barrage of opinion and profanity to enforce her point that I was not a legitimate heir. My Mother yelled, "Joan how could you do this to me", and ran into her bedroom slamming the door. I had heard enough; I went into the living room and grabbed Joan by the arm and pulled her into the second bedroom off the living room and shut the door. I told her to shut up or I would throw her out of the house if she uttered one more word. Joan and my cousins Craig and Jerry left soon thereafter. I found that apparently all my relatives, with the exceptions of the Edgar Boehner family, my Cousin Zandra, and my Uncle Vernon, considered me a tolerated member of the family, but not relation per se. After Dad's death, I maintained sporadic contact with family, but the contact ended upon Sidonia's passing in 2010 and I am rejected now by the family as a whole. I went on with my career in law enforcement, private investigation, and eventually civil and criminal law as a paralegal spanning thirty-one years.

In December 2004, Sidonia suffered congestive heart failure followed by two limited and recoverable strokes in January 2005. The illness left her in dementia and unable to care for herself and in February we moved Mom into our home to care for her. During the following months we cared for Mom, to her every need, want, and desire. I retired from my in-home business and my wife Lucretia retired from retail as it took both of us to provide assistance to Sidonia. But as Sidonia recovered physically she became increasingly aggressive in her attitude and demeanor towards us. She would spend hours on the telephone telling friends and relatives how mean and cruel we were, forcing medicine on her, making her eat awful food, and making her take her medicine. She refused to call Lucretia by her name, instead calling her "that woman". On a number of occasions, Sidonia seriously attacked Lucretia with her cane. Mom actually pleaded with me to "get the shotgun and just shoot her". By May 2005 Mom had recovered enough to make a trip to Southern California to visit Joan Moiola and was cleared by her physician Dr. Rice to make the trip. Sidonia stayed with Joan to the end of August, coming back with a whole new attitude, apparently that Lucretia and I were crooks, as Sidonia then began telling everyone we had "stolen her money and left her penniless". She continued with her false and degrading phone calls to anyone who would listen.

Sidonia's recovery, by September 2005 was estimated at 85-90%, and we felt it was time Mom go to a retirement home due to her increasing hostility towards us. We discussed the issues with her to which she agreed it was time. Together we selected a very nice retirement home in Visalia, took Mom over to meet the staff and review the accommodations, and she decided on her own volition to move into the apartment at Walnut Glen. We had also talked about her home in Visalia which she had purchased from proceeds from the sale of the ranch in Exeter in 1987. I told Sidonia of the pending crisis in the housing market and that I thought it would be best to get the house cleaned out and placed on the market. I contacted a realtor friend whom I had done paralegal work for and who had helped us purchase and sell a recent house. Mom agreed and after she was moved into the apartment, Lucretia and I began cleaning the house and packing her remaining household goods. On a Sunday morning in late October, Lucretia and I went over to her home to continue cleaning and packing up her household goods. Upon our arrival we noticed a locksmith's truck parked outside and my Cousin Shane, coming out the front door with a box of possessions. We found that someone had convinced my Mother, or actually vice versa, that we were stealing all her things and that we should be prevented from all access to the house. At the time, we found Mom sitting in the spare bedroom, refusing to speak or even look at us. Lucretia and I walked out of the house and never returned. Sidonia ignored my advice to list the property and eventually sold at a $175K loss. Between September and December 2005, Lucretia and I sold our home in Visalia, purchasing a small ranch in Hot Springs, South Dakota. This act was the last straw for Sidonia, and she reminded me of my promise to care for her forever. I told her we still loved her, would care for her and help her as she needed, but the affirmation fell on deaf ears.

The ultimate betrayal came on December 2, 2005. While we were getting ready to leave for South Dakota, Sidonia driven by my Uncle Vernon, pulled up to the curb in front of our house. Mom stepped out of the car and approached Lucretia and I standing on the sidewalk and flatly stated, "Thank you for making my life so miserable". Sidonia re-entered the car and they drove away. That was the last time we saw her; we never spoke again. Sidonia removed me from her Will and as Power of Attorney in her Living Trust, ensuring I was no longer her Son. She passed away in Reno, Nevada on February 10, 2010, a lonely and bitter woman, believing she was taking my adoption history, birth name, and parents' names to her grave rather than reveal for my benefit. But she was wrong as I had already received the unintentional information two years before from my daughter Kimberly.

The worst fear of my Mother was that the relatives would take my inheritance, when in fact it would be she who would insure they did get it. The relatives picked over what was there of any value. What belonged to me as personal pictures, mementos, Vietnam era keepsakes, and grade school year books, pictures, clothes, dresser, and memories from various articles went to the trash, sold, or given away without a second thought. Except for several items of my Father and an antique photo album from my Grandmother Labahn, I hold nothing from my past before 1988. It is like I never existed.

CHAPTER 5

DISCOVERIES

In November 2008, I received an email from my daughter Kimberly stating that while she was sitting with my Mother going through some of her old papers, she accidentally found an envelope containing my Order For Adoption. She told me my birth name and the names of my Mother and Father listed on the form. Initially, I was elated as now I had actual names on which I could search; but elation soon turned to anger as the realization set in that my adoptive parents knew of my identity all this time and willfully chose to hide it from me until after their deaths. It was a punch in the gut, a slap in the face, and the last straw in the relationship with my adoptive mother, and family. I did not have the opportunity to discuss my discovery with her. To do so would require revealing where the information came from thus placing my daughter in a very difficult position, damaging her relationship with Sidonia; I kept the revelation quiet.

It was all I needed to begin finding my birth family in Tennessee. Kim mailed me the documents and I wasted no time in firing off a letter to the Department of Children's Services, Post Adoption Unit, 436 – 6th Avenue, NW, 8th Floor Cordell Hull Building, Nashville, Tennessee 37243-1290. I found the process unclear, over-burdened with red tape, and requiring multiple contacts and clarifications before the department would even admit to having any record. It would take me until May 6, 2009, before receiving my case file documents from Tennessee. I didn't wait for the files. By December 2008, I was online with Ancestry.com, a genealogical research fee-based website. As an investigator and paralegal, I found Ancestry a wonderful research tool. I was able to access records and information with just a click of the mouse, versus the 'old days' of trudging to the Clerk's Office or other information sources to get a Clerk's assistance to find and copy a case or form. Within a day of entering in my adoptive parents' names, I was tracking my Lenard Arnold Harris family, finding U.S. Census reports, military induction records, birth and marriage records, and the identification of my Grandparents lineage going back to the 13th Century. My birth mother Flossie Louise Bowman turned out to be a whole other adventure.

What I did not have was Flossie's middle name, only an 'L' was listed on the adoption order. One would think that the name 'Flossie' would be somewhat rare, especially when targeted to one specific, small geographical area. Not the case in Tennessee; I found dozens upon dozens of Flossie L. Bowman's of record in Tennessee, Georgia, Alabama, and Mississippi. Each name was reviewed, researched, saved or discarded based upon Census, age, race, and locations of residence in 1949. It was a long, tedious search but eventually was reduced to one possible name, a lady named Mary Virginia Flossa Lee Bowman. Mary, who went commonly by the name 'Flossie', had lived in the Whitwell-Jasper area during my specific time period and was a member of the Aud Bowman family, now scattered from western Tennessee to Las Vegas, and Michigan. It was said that Mary had been named after all her father's girlfriends. From a newspaper obituary, I obtained names of living relatives whom had attended Aud Bowman's funeral and with the help of internet people search programs, located the children of Flossie Bowman. I contacted the Bowman family historian Brenda Messer living in North Carolina and found the following history documented by her, in part:

Mary was born in Tennessee and was 24 years old in 1949. She was identified as a "free spirit" and one who lived her life as she much desired. As a young woman, she worked as a barmaid in a honky tonk saloon in Sequachie, Tennessee, drank heavily and had a habit of disappearing for months at a time. In mid-1949, Mary was pregnant from an unknown suitor, and was forced by her Mother-In-Law to board a train for an unknown destination to have the child in secret. We surmised it may have been to a 'birthing clinic' operated by the Tennessee Children's Home Society, and very possibly Wright's Clinic in Jasper. We could only guess in that she gave birth and the child was immediately surrendered for adoption, or stolen by the TCHS. Facts were coming together, but not to a definitive conclusion. I was put in contact with my possible siblings and information was flowing in supporting the theory of them being my lost family. The identification of a sister in May 2009, an apparent match with Linda Henry Nicholson of Las Vegas, Nevada, seemed to cement the correlation together as the TCHS notated a child "Linda" born in 1947 to Flossie. As I read through the case files sent by Tennessee, information poured from the pages, bolstering the opinion this family was the right Bowman clan. Through the remainder of 2009 we enjoyed weekly emails back and forth between the siblings and basically getting to know one another. In February 2010, I found just how wrong a person can be.

On a cold, snowy morning I was sitting at the desk working on Ancestry. com leads on the Bowman family line. As I reverted back to the family tree page I received a "Leaf" indicating a new lead on Flossie. Clicking on the Leaf revealed it was a Social Security Death document for Flossie Louise Bowman of Whitwell, Tennessee, but not the same number and birth date as Mary Virginia; I thought I had exhausted every Flossie Bowman on the planet. I returned to the Home Page of Ancestry and decided, due to the discovery of Arnold Griffith's name, to develop a new search and list Arnold as the Father, and Flossie Louise as the Mother. That was the combination, the right combination. Within hours, I received my first message from who would turn out to be my Cousin Jeffi White living in Griffith Creek, Tennessee. As weeks and months progressed, information was pouring in from relatives and my internet research, but the information on my Mother Flossie was the most astounding and the correlation with Mary Virginia, here in part:

Flossie Louise Bowman was born January 15, 1929, to Joseph Bowman and Nancy Jane Kilgore in Whitwell, Marion County, Tennessee. Her father was a coal miner, a drinker, but not much of a gambler, surviving on a dirt-poor income. Joe was very secretive about his past and is rumored to have left Alabama one step ahead of the law for some unknown misdeed, changing his name from Trullis or Trullius to Bowman. He was also a rough character, accounted in two separate newspaper articles of gun battles; one at his home in Whitwell, and another in downtown Jasper, Tennessee.

At about age 15 Flossie went to work as a barmaid at a little honky tonk saloon in Sequachie, Tennessee not far from Whitwell. She met Lenard Arnold Harris of Tracy City, Tennessee, a frequent patron whose off-work passions were drinking and gambling. One thing quickly led to another and Flossie and Lenard were married on 25 June 1945 in Catoosa County, Ringgold, Georgia, as recorded in Book L Page 478 Ordinary's Office. When working Lenard was a migrant farm worker and in turn a self-made businessman. Lenard owned a truck and followed the seasonal fruit and vegetable harvests from Florida and Georgia up to the Ohio Valley, hard back-breaking work (for a person with a spine deformity). He would gather lug boxes of citrus consisting mainly of oranges, lemons, tangerines, and peaches and transport along his seasonal route to trade for vegetables grown in the northern states. When the northern picking season was over Lenard would return through Illinois and back to Tennessee, selling his vegetables along the way. Flossie accompanied Lenard on one or two of these trips but quickly found the farm worker life was not for her and the couple separated in late 1946.

Flossie returned to Whitwell from Tracy City and also returned to her old job at the Sequachie bar. In early 1947, Flossie met Arnold Lafayette Griffith of Griffith Creek, Tennessee, currently on leave from the U.S. Army. As with the other men in Flossie's life, Arnold was a drinker which seemed to keep him in perpetual trouble with the military police and local authorities. Arnold enjoyed being a Private with as little responsibility as possible. Repeated attempts to promote Private Griffith usually resulted in the closest Officer being slugged and Arnold, nicknamed 'Cotton' by the family due to his white/blonde hair, on his way to the guardhouse being held to the rank of Private once again.

In December 1947, Flossie gave birth to Linda Jane Griffith with Arnold as her declared Father. Flossie was dependent upon Arnold's monthly allotments he would send from Fort Jackson in South Carolina, but a Private's salary was meager at best, and Flossie was forced to seek assistance from Marion County Social Welfare for Linda. To help ease her financial deficit, Flossie reluctantly returned to her job at the bar and also moved in with her sister Josie in Whitwell. At 19 years old, the impoverished atmosphere in Whitwell, Tennessee would become her lot in life. She once again became pregnant and in May 1949 gave birth to James Arnold Bowman at Wright's Clinic, in Jasper.

Flossie wanted this child for several reasons; first, she needed the additional welfare money amounting to about Ten Dollars extra per month; second, she realized with another child, Arnold would also garnish a small raise, having two dependent children, thus sending more money home each month; and third, the stated fact in her own words in her letter dated May 20, 1949, that she would never give one of her babies away; Flossie did not believe in adoption, she didn't have too. Arnold Griffith had seven surviving siblings in 1949, and one in particular Ms. Onnie Griffith would serve as the family matron and caregiver to a majority of the family children. My sister Linda was raised by Onnie from early childhood, as was my brother Eddie Arnold Griffith who lived with Onnie off and on until his death in 2011. At the time of Onnie's passing in December 2012, she was caring for my nephew, Jeremiah Griffith of Griffith Creek. The Griffith family never learned of my birth or alleged death, but if known would have intervened in the adoption. My Aunt Onnie did mention to Linda of a baby dying, believing it was actually me.

I discovered through my research that Flossie and Arnold were married in June 1951 at the Courthouse in Rossville, Georgia. I believe Arnold and

Flossie had a tinge of conscious, desiring to be married before the birth of Eddie Arnold Griffith on August 25, 1951. I sadly found that the young Griffith couple were not 'Ozzie & Harriet'. As two wolves in a cave, their alcohol binges fueled repeated fights, occassionally with firearms, and absence of one spouse or the other for weeks at a time. Conditions led to Linda and Eddie being received by Onnie Griffith to essentially raise as her own children. Linda and Eddie drifted away from contact with Flossie and Arnold, never to be readdressed. Arnold Lafayette Griffith died on 29 May 1978 from injuries sustained in an auto accident. Some relatives say the incident was intentional, caused by some undesireables wanting Arnold dead for some believed transgression. The local police did not see any evidence of foul play; no investigation was launched. It is possible that Arnold was never told of my existance.

Following Arnold's death, Flossie Bowman continued with her lifestyle at the local bars, but in more sober moments maintained a limited relationship with the Charles Kilgore family, as related to our Grandmother Nancy Jane Kilgore Bowman Mosier of Whitwell, Tennessee. Flossie remarried shortly before her passing to a gentleman named Harold Little. Virtually nothing is known of Mr. Little, disappearing after Flossie's death. Flossie's lifestyle took its toll bringing on diabetes and the effects of long-term consumption. Flossie Louise Bowman Little passed away in Marion County, Whitwell, Tennessee on July 26, 1993. Flossie never knew I survived.

My sister Linda and brother Eddie were raised mostly by our Aunt Oma Griffith who loved and cared for them as her own. Linda went on to be a professional with a local credit union and still lives at Griffith Creek. Eddie eventually succombed to a life of alcohol abuse, dying of a severe brain hemorage while doing business at his sister's credit union. Thankfully Linda was not working that day.

In February 2013 DNA sample kits were performed and activated through AncestryDNA services for paternity verification. The results came back quickly in March. In sample saliva testing with my uncle Eb Griffith of Griffith Creek, Tennessee, the results were positive to a 99 percentile, that Arnold Lafayette Griffith is my biological father.

The feeling I have in finding my biological family is beyond words. The chance of my search being successful was millions to one, let alone finding relatives who recall my birth, and alleged demise. I am very sad for the Henry family who believed they had found a lost brother and I a lost family. Even though it turned out differently, I will always consider the Henry brothers and sisters part of my Bowman clan. I am sorrowful I could not find my parents to tell them I was alright or to have the opportunity to ask the real story as they would recall it; and, yes I am angry on a whole host of issues that would keep psychologists busy for a decade. Even into 2013 where in a letter I appealed for assistance to the Department of Children's Services in Nashville, for review of my adoption and its revocation, their response was basically 'nothing we can do, good luck with that.' I am not a believer in luck . . . if I was lucky, I'd be rich and handsome; instead they get old and determined.

My story is not new. Thousands of children were ripped from their parents love and care and scattered to the four winds, siblings separated and never knowing the other existed. Names, birth data, parents names, all changed for the sole purpose of keeping the child secret and available for sale while the parents were left with no one to take their cause. Imagine your child stolen from you, and no one cares at all; no report, no investigation, no justice. I remember a story that my adoptive mother told about an incident on a trip to Orange, California. My mother stopped at a shop in Orange and ran in for just a minute, leaving me in the car. She glanced out the shop window and saw a man trying to entice me to pull up the door knob. She ran from the shop in horror and the man ran off down the street. She never left me in the car alone again. It is that feeling the parents must have felt as their child(ren) were being taken forcifully from them by Social Workers and the TCHS . . . no report, no investigation, no justice.

How is it that a couple who wants children so bad as to adopt a child under suspicious and questionable circumstances, elects to keep the details secret until both are dead, regardless of possible ramifications by and to the adopted child? My adoptive parents were not stupid. They knew something was terribly wrong with my adoption; hence the secrecy. They were willing and complacent in not considering that a mother and father were without their child. *"The child was neglected and abandoned by the parents."*, Alma Walton would have told them, as she did with countless other Southern California adoptive parents. We moved rapidly in succession from Temple City to Fullerton in 1952, to La Habra in 1954, and finally to Exeter in 1957; the last two addresses were never on file with the TCHS or Social Services. It was wrong of them to keep the details of my adoption from me after I turned of age. It was wrong of me not to ask in fear of hurting my mother's feelings.

Being a chapter entitled 'Discovery' I believe it has been a discovery of self moreso than facts and bloodlines. Knowing where one comes from is an important part of who we are today, and why we may have tendancies towards different likes or dislikes, physical traits, or history of illness or disease. I have found patriotic Americans in our history, from the Mayflower through the Revolution, the Civil War and WWII. I also found a content Great-Grandfather whose sole joy was sitting on the porch of his log cabin, dog at his feet, with a jar of moonshine in hand. I have found that living relatives are like jewels, so very precious in their memories, stories, photographs, and their recollections of life 'back then'. These documentatians of history must have their words preserved and passed down to following generations. My father and grandfather worked in the coal mines under the town of Griffith Creek. Each morning they would walk the eight miles down the mountain to enter the mines, and each evening walk the eight miles back home after a back-breaking day digging and hauling coal. It was work, even if only a Dollar Fifty a day. It is these stories which give an understanding to the character of the times and why choices were made that are hard to comprehend today.

My search for my family is finished and my quest of knowing my story is successful. Now it is time to focus on the last remaining detail . . . justice. Where does one start to gain justice? Where any inquiry begins . . . with Investigation and Evidence.

CHAPTER 6

INVESTIGATION AND EVIDENCE

". . . when you have eliminated the impossible, whatever remains
however improbable, must be the truth".
Sherlock Holmes—*"The Sign of Four"*
by *Arthur Conan Doyle*

It is a difficult and challenging undertaking to resurrect a 65 year old abduction case where virtually all witnesses are elderly or deceased. It is imperative for any investigator or researcher to remain impartial and view the facts and related history as the evidence documents, not as what seems to be under the light of scrutiny; a hard task when the abduction is your own.

The Reader has been provided narrative, witnesses, photographs, and actual documents from the period in question as well as history of the principle organization involved in the alleged abduction and cover-up of true events outlined in the pages of correspondence between Tennessee Children's Home Society, Marion County Social Welfare, and Wright's Clinic. We have become familiar with the main cast of characters involved at this alleged crime scene beginning at Wright's Clinic and their testimony thus documented in their own words. We have evidence from the biological mother in her own handwriting and a latter paper trail indicating a possible conspiracy involving the major principals to steal an infant child and sell for profit, concealed by contrived, illegal adoption proceedings sanctioned by the states of Tennessee and California. We have uncovered living relatives who know of the victim in 1949 and provide the first, and only, declaration recounting the reported death of the child while at Wright's Clinic. We have everything we need and what is possible under the given circumstances and restraints of time and history, to possess Probable Cause to initiate an investigation into crimes alleged. Consider the following case history scenario – You are the Investigator:

Case History Study ~

Proposed criminal and civil violations:

- Child Abduction/Kidnapping
- Unlawful Sale of a Child for Profit
- Grand Theft and Extortion Upon Adoptive Parents by Unlawful Adoption Scam
- False Imprisonment and Concealment of Child Under Color of Authority
- Unlawful Removal of a Child Across State Lines Under Color of Authority
- Fraudulent preparation of TN and CA state documents
- Forgery of maternal signatures and specific correspondences
- Conspiracy to commit multiple Felonies
- Obstruction of Justice
- Violation of Tennessee and California adoption laws
- Violation of Parents and Child's Civil Rights, and
- Applicable Civil Torts

Elements necessary to frame the criminal case:

- Means: Suspects maintained the legal knowledge, position, cash, and technical means to carry out the crimes alleged.
- Method: Suspects maintained decades of expertise in concealing over 5,000 stolen children, preparing false documents and records, and completing illegal adoptions.
- Opportunity: Under false Color of Authority by corruption, the TCHS and Wright's Clinic maintained complete opportunity to initiate and complete the criminal conduct as alleged.
- Mens Rea: The principal Suspects maintained the mental and conscious state knowing that the actions being performed by them were illegal under existing Tennessee and federal laws, and contrary to sound moral judgment.
- Primary Document and Physical Evidence List:

- **(Fig. 1)** *Certificate_of_Live_Birth_141-49-28302_(June_13,_1949)*: Document handwritten in script using a fountain pen and black ink onto plain stock typing paper. Certificate unsigned by delivering physician Dr. McMillian; witnessed by Steven Bryar (6/13/49). Certificate missing information normally found on standard birth certificates. Certificate number does not correspond with TN state-issued number sequence and was not prepared on the recorded birthdate of May 8, 1949. It is surmised that Bryar prepared the certificate out of presence of Dr. McMillian or vice versa; the entire certificate is in one person's script.

- **(Fig. 8)** *Certificate_of_Live_Birth_141-49-25202_(June_8,_1949)*: Document is a standard Tennessee state Form 100 Certificate of Live Birth and typewritten. Line 20B reflects information for the certificate, and preparation thereof, was completed on June 8, 1949. The certificate bears child's adoptive name and parents' names; also a residential address in Fullerton, CA, the Boehner's would not have until 1952. This document could not have been received or prepared by the Registrar (Acting), Department of Public Health, Division of Vital Statistics, M.R. Baird declared in 1949. The document is associated with a request dated September 9, 1952 from the TCHS to the Boehner's new address in Fullerton, CA, asking they fill out and submit (2) TN 181A forms so a new Birth Certificate could be made. The Certificate number recorded and issued by the state is substantially lower than the 1949 handwritten Bryar document. It is also noted that the area at the bottom of the certificate entitled "For Medical and Health Use Only" is blocked out with tape. This certificate is fraudulent, null and void on its face, and of no force and effect.

- **(Fig. 4)** *First_Letter_from_TCHS_to_Bowman_(May_16,_1949)*: Copy of onion-skin business format letter typewritten in Courier typeset with no type abnormalities identified. First written document from Margaret Hall, Field Secretary (TCHS), expressing an interest to adopt James Arnold Bowman (victim). Prepared on plain stock typing paper with no letterhead.

- *Investigative_Note*: All copies of letters received from the TN Adoptions Unit, displaying originating correspondence from the TCHS (Hall), appear to be copies of 'onion-skin copies' of the actual letters, void of all signatures. All original letters are absent from the official TCHS file now held in Nashville, Department of Children's Services. It is undetermined as to why and how onion-skin copies, normally retained by the person preparing the correspondence, were recovered in the files of the recipients in Chattanooga, Memphis, and Nashville.

- *(Fig. 5) First Letter from Bowman to TCHS (May 20, 1949)*: Copy of a personal letter handwritten in pencil in script on standard lined writing tablet paper 4"x7". First correspondence from Flossie Bowman to Margaret Hall, Field Secretary, TCHS. Presents Bowman's flat refusal of adoption services to TCHS. No evidence has been received to indicate this letter was not written and signed by Flossie Bowman. It is further noted that a staple duplication is identified in the upper-left corner of the letter but without evidence of what may have been attached or by whom.

- *Investigative Note*: The above letter copy has been used for handwriting comparison against all other available writings and signatures of Flossie Bowman. The only close match was accorded to the letter of December 1, 1949, but not written and signed by the same person.

- *(Fig. 6) Letter from Margaret Hall to Mary Hawkins Wright (May 25, 1945)*: Copy of onion-skin business format letter typewritten in Courier typeset with no type abnormalities identified. This letter confirms receipt of Flossie Bowman's letter of May 20th refusing offer of adoption services from the TCHS.

- *Lapsed Time From May 25th to September 30, 1949*: During this period, there was no documented contact between the parties involved.

- *Investigative Note*: In the "Child's Own History" case sheet prepared by Margaret Hall on December 26, 1949, Miss Hall states, in part, ". . ." In September (1949) Flossie returned the baby to Wright's Hospital. Dr. McMillian found it to be undernourished and suffering with diarrhea. He ordered the mother to take it to Children's Hospital in Chattanooga. It was admitted with a diagnosis of infectious diarrhea. Again Ms. W. (Wright) encouraged the mother to release the baby but she refused to do it." The document also relates to the child being brought to Wright's Clinic by Bowman on November 15, 1949. The lapsed time is important as there was a lot of activity allegedly involving the victim's health, but without supporting documents of hospital check-in, authorizations and releases, or indication of a plan of prognosis treatment. The time void is also important when considering the following letter from Georgia Tann on September 30, 1949.

- *(Fig. 9) Letter from Georgia Tann to Walter and Sidonia Boehner (September 30, 1949)*: Copy of onion-skin business format letter typewritten in Courier format typeset with an abnormality of displaced letters and 'wavy' sentences possibly caused by a loose roller on the manual typewriter used. The letter was void of any letterhead. The letter confirms to the victim's future adoptive parents they had been accepted for placement of a child and would be notified when the proper child was available. The letter also cautions them not to attempt personal pick-up of the child but to rather have the child delivered to them.

- *Investigative Notes*: The September 30th letter from Tann is highly suspicious on two points; first, how was this letter associated to my adoption file 'if' a child had not become available at that time; and secondly, if the 'Child's Own Family case history is to be believed, the date of November 15th where Flossie brings the child to Wright's Hospital is very close to Tann's letter noted above. There is no documentation of the Boehner's initial request for adoption services through the TCHS or documentation of any 'prescreening or evaluation' efforts to approve them for placement. Such assignments and completion would not be performed until Summer 1952, by Mrs. Natalia Tachekoloff, California Department of Social Services. It could be argued that Flossie brought the child into Wright's Clinic and left same for treatment in September 1949, never to see the child again because 'the child died and remains taken care of', as related by witness family relatives Hazel Kilgore and Glenda Waldon. Documentation suggests the TCHS was specifically aware of the victim as of May 8, 1949, and targeted the victim for adoption legal or otherwise through the use of hired and paid "Spotters" Mary Hawkins Wright and Margaret Hall. When Bowman refused adoption services, plans of the TCHS were set in motion to steal the child and create the fraudulent foundation for adoption. On March 3, 2013, a telephone check with the Records Division, T.J. Thompson Hospital, Chattanooga, Tennessee, could not verify the victim's admission for treatment in 1949; records are destroyed 10 years after closure of treatment.

- *(Fig. 10) Letter from Margaret Hall to Bowman (October 24, 1949)*: Copy of onion-skin business format letter typewritten in Courier typeset and void of type abnormalities or letterhead. This letter is very suspicious as it responds to an undocumented occurrence where Bowman allegedly expresses her sudden interest in "plans for the baby" to an unidentified third person who in turn notifies Hall. The letter further indicates that Bowman is still in possession of the child and ". . . could you take the baby to Mrs. Wright and meet me there sometime?" It is unclear whether Hall is relating to 'adoption' or to 'financial arrangements' as was made a concern in Margaret Hall's letter of November 21, 1949.

- *Investigative Notes*: At face value, the letter appears as a simple follow-up to an apparent change-of-heart by Bowman to adopt out the child. But, when combined with forthcoming letters interchanging between Bowman and the Tennessee Children's Home Society Field Representative Margaret Hall, the appearance of propriety fades rapidly. The Bowman letters of October 31, December 1ˢᵗ (a close partial match), December 7, and, the Surrender document signature of December 8, 1949 are blatant forgeries. Examination of the handwriting compared with Bowman's letter of May 20, 1949 does not match in composition, spelling, sentence structure or style. When contrasting events from September 15ᵗʰ through December 8, 1949, it is possible to suggest that the Hall letters from as early as October 24ᵗʰ were prepared and never intended to be sent to Bowman; that the Bowman letters in alleged responses were drafted by an unknown conspirator to appear as such, for the sole purpose of providing a false paper trail leading to the child being surrendered on December 8ᵗʰ.

- *(Fig. 16) Surrender To Tennessee Children's Home Society (December 8, 1949)*: Copy of a preprinted legal-size form executed in Courier typeset, and two forms of fountain pens with different stylus points. The notarized form does not bear any notary stamps and the handwritten name of the Notary is unreadable. The signature of Flossie Louise Bowman is a forgery and does not match the example of Bowman's handwriting of May 20ᵗʰ; there is a pencil tracing visible under the ink signature of the "F" as well as 'pauses and stops' in the signature as the person attempted to trace in ink a light pre-patterned signature done in pencil first. The document is a forgery, null and void on its face, and of no force and effect.

- *Investigative Notes*: This TCHS form is the Holy Grail of case documents and the item most necessary to proceed for an out-of-state adoption. A parent or guardian signature is required for the sole purpose of preventing trafficking in stolen children, and the action of such proceedings not being able to be conducted covertly; the Notary is present to insure the person signing is in fact the proper person as identified. This form depicts that the major part of the form, including Bowman's signature, is performed with a fountain pen with a broad, worn stylus and older ink, whereas the witness signatures of Swofford and Mary Hawkins Wright, used a different fountain pen with a sharper stylus and fresh ink. It can be surmised that witnesses signed at a different time using different pens. A well-known legal doctrine can be applied in this case known as the "Fruit of the Poisoned Tree". When something is derived from a source which is concluded to be unlawful, then everything derived from that source is also unlawful and cannot be used as so intended in a court of law. I assert the doctrine applies in this case. The mere presentation of this all-important document, in this condition, should have brought this matter to a screeching halt until further review or correction; neither occurred.

Circumstantial Considerations:

There is no evidence to prove correspondence originating from Margaret Hall between October 24th and December 2, 1949 were ever mailed, and in fact, supported by forged Bowman responses, the letters were not sent. In placing the Tennessee Children's Home Society's history of falsifying hundreds of adoptions into consideration, it would be a small step to observe direct and calculated actions by Wright and Hall to prepare a 'limited' paper trail obviously leading to the surrender signing. Bowman was unaware of the interest and subsequent actions being taken by Hall and Wright to steal the child on behalf of Georgia Tann and the TCHS.

There is no evidence to support the written claim that the child was taken to Thompson Hospital in Chattanooga due to acute illness in November 1949, or that treatment was provided at Wright's Clinic in Jasper in September 1949. The child was stated to have been born 2 months premature and remained in Wright's Hospital for an undocumented period of time until the child weighed six pounds, from the original birth weight of three pounds. The child was released to Bowman but shortly thereafter allegedly developed an acute gastrointestinal infection diagnosed by Dr. McMillian at Wright's Clinic. The child was left for examination and evaluation at Wright's Clinic about September 15, 1949, according to Hall's own statement written December 26, 1949. Witnesses Hazel Kilgore and Glenda Waldon recall being told that Flossie's baby died but cannot remember the time of year or surrounding circumstances of the event, being children themselves at that time.

If the story surrounding the child's illness and treatment is to be believed, observation of the illness and treatment as available in 1949 must be made as well. The limited description of the related illness affecting the child is believed to be a form of *Gastroenteritis* described as "a condition that causes irritation and inflammation of the stomach and intestines". Symptoms would include vomiting, diarrhea, dehydration, and weight loss. Penicillin may have been administered if considered a viral infection, but primary treatment would have concentrated on fluids, bland foods, and rest to regain strength and body weight. The child may have gained slightly since birth, but predictably not more than a pound by September 1949 due to illness, and could reasonably have lost any gain due to the illness. To reach the reported goal of six pounds to initiate release, and be in Flossie Bowman's personal custody before November 17th to be released to Wright's Clinic for "observation and evaluation", the child would have to recover from the illness and gain a minimum of three pounds in under 2 months. Prior care does not support this thesis. The Examinations and Recommendations Record of December 9 through December 13, 1949 as prepared by the Chattanooga TCHS stated the child still suffered from symptoms but was still authorized for release by the unidentified physician attending. It should be inserted here that the child's adoptive mother took him to her family physician in Pasadena, California, in approximately late January 1950. The physician reported verbally ". . . the child is very dehydrated, malnourished, and suffering with vomiting, diarrhea, and congestion. If I were you (Mrs. Boehner), and I didn't know how much you wanted this child, I would tell you to send him back." It is improbable that TJ Thompson Hospital released the child without a full, reasonable recovery from the illness. The alleged recorded weight of the child on December 9, 1949, was 12 pounds fourteen ounces. As of February 15, 1950, the child's recorded weight was sixteen pounds four ounces. The lack of prognosis care between September and December 1949 seems to dictate that a regional hospital was not involved in the treatment of the baby, only possibly Wright's Hospital on the initial assessment alleged in September 1949. The stated birth weight was artificially inflated to promote release.

In further consideration, the history and known actions of the victim's mother must be included as circumstantial interest. Bowman was already a parent when the victim was born in May 1949, was in custody and care of her daughter, and receiving aid from Marion County, and from her companion Arnold Griffith for the existing child. Bowman had no history of desiring to adopt out their daughter Linda Jane Griffith born December 1947, or, their son Eddie Arnold Griffith born to them in 1951. Bowman told Hall and Wright she had no desire to use their services. When the victim was born, Bowman also applied for aid to also cover the new child. Being concerned about the new baby, naming the child after his father, taking the child for health treatment(s), and outwardly debunking any adoption help are not the actions of a mother wanting to rid herself of a premature, sick child as the TCHS subtly suggests.

In the process of Tennessee adoptions at the time the adoption case is filed with the Court of jurisdiction, the parent(s) or legal guardian are required to be served notice (Summons and Petition) that an action is pending against them. In this case, process service was performed by publication, but no Proof of Service is present with the Tennessee portion of the filing. Normally on a service by publication, a legal notice is published in the newspaper 'most likely' to provide notice to the Defendant(s) for a set number of days and to include a copy of the action mailed to the Defendant's last known address. Once service is completed the Proof of Service by Publication is prepared and filed; the case then proceeds upon its legal requirements and merit. If service of process is found to have been performed in a Nashville newspaper, it can be argued that process service was not completed in a manner most likely to give proper notice, therefore the Defendant(s) were not properly notified of the action against them, not given the opportunity to answer the Summons, and creating the legal premise for the State to enter a Default Judgment upon such non-appearance by Defendant(s).

We close our investigative study in the essential clues, documents and history thus offering the following Investigative Synopsis of events:

Investigative Synopsis ~

There is no 'official' document or related witness verifying the date of birth as May 8, 1949. The handwritten Certificate of Live Birth is void of specific birth record and information and was not certified by the notated Steven Bryar until June 13, 1949. The certificate was never signed by the delivering physician McMillian. As with documented history of the TCHS, the alternate date may have been selected to derail any latter inquiries into the child's birth. This probability supports the actions of Hall and Wright in their quick interest of the newborn, why the preparation of a birth certificate may have been intentionally delayed to attempt cooperation from Bowman, and the anger felt by Wright and Hall when Bowman would not conform. The child was selected by Mary Hawkins Wright, after birth, as a target for illegal adoption following Bowman's refusal to concede. It is possible the correct date of birth is actually June 13, 1949.

It was now up to Wright and Hall to establish the groundwork for the planned adoption. It is not the first illegal adoption the pair had worked on and they knew from experience, and from instruction from Georgia Tann, of exactly what would be needed in advance. Their first opportunity occurred after several medical visits by Bowman, bringing in the sick infant for care for the last time in September 1949, leaving the baby for "treatment and evaluation". It is the exact scenario the TCHS hoped for, an open invitation to take the child. There is no credible information or document which indicates Bowman ever saw her child again. It is asserted that during the following period between late September and November 15, 1949, Flossie Bowman was informed by Wright or Hall that her baby had succumbed to his illness and died; Flossie was not to worry as Wright's Clinic would take care of the remains for her. It was a standard line given to a majority of unwed mothers whose infants were stolen. They would wait for a short period of time to see if any inquiries were raised then secret the victim from the Clinic to the Chattanooga TCHS orphanage; out of sight, out of mind.

First, letters of contact had to be developed between the clinic, TCHS, and Bowman, providing the paper trail leading to an obvious and necessary surrender for adoption. These tasks were accomplished aided by forged, handwritten documents poorly written in Bowman's name; so poorly written in fact that Margaret Hall addressed the matter in her Child's Own History narrative of December 26, 1949, stating that the letters were not written by Bowman but apparently by someone else. The series of letters brought the tentative adoption to the Surrender form of December 8, 1949. Georgia Tann's letter of September 30, 1949 to the Boehner's informing them they had been selected for placement inadvertently reveals the process already underway by that date. There is no plausible way in which Tann could have associated the Boehner family to this child's file, unless selection had already been done. The leading result of this factual information is that the victim was most likely removed from Wright's Clinic by Margaret Hall between the dates of September 15-30, 1949, and secreted to the Chattanooga orphanage of the TCHS. The blatant admission by Hall of the mismatched handwriting was expertly used to disparage Bowman's original letter of May 20th, thus disparaging any conceived Bowman denial of TCHS services, casting doubt thereto upon Flossie's personal belief against adoption. Supported by letters allegedly un-mailed by Hall and Wright, and responses not executed in Bowman's handwriting, the final leg of the illegal adoption scam was in sight.

On a cold December day, Hall and Wright met at Wright's Clinic in Jasper to finalize the illegal adoption surrender form; the only known persons missing from the event were Flossie Bowman and the victim. Examination of the surrender form identifies a complete forgery as clearly represented by the pencil-traced signature represented to be Bowman's signature by her own hand. The form was witnessed by an unknown person named Howard G. Swofford, and the ever-present and helpful Mary Hawkins Wright. The form and signature would be used as the basis for all remaining adoption criteria's, and the Order for a new Certificate of Live Birth in both Tennessee and California, in the name of Donald Walter Boehner. The victim was secreted from Chattanooga to Georgia Tann's home in Memphis, then from Memphis to Nashville in the company of a Mrs. (Alma) Walton, and by mid-January 1950 was transported by train in the charge of Alma Watson to the Biltmore Hotel, Los Angeles, California, and given to the victim's adoptive parents upon completion of payment of the arranged 'fee' of $5,000.00 total as told by the adoptive mother Sidonia.

There are no physical documents relating to how the adoptive parents were referred to the attorney firm of Hooper & Miller of Los Angeles, who are known and identified as a conspirator with Georgia Tann, or if they were referred at all. On the civil adoption in California, no signatures appear anywhere to affirm the Boehner's ever saw George A. Hooper, the Lead Partner of the firm who prepared the necessary forms and signed on their behalf. Searches conducted in 2009, 2011, 2012 and 2014 by the Orange County Superior Court to locate the court file number A-22307 and the accompanying allegedly filed Order of March 4, 1953, could not find a case file of record. Hooper new of the contrived legal status of the adoption as he had performed a number of them before for Smiley Burnette, June Allison, and the gangster Frank Netti among others. For the right money, he maintained the means, method, opportunity and especially the mens rea (state of mind) to commit the crimes alleged. It is surmised that Hooper was paid directly by Tann for his 'service fee' upon the assignment of the adoption case. It made perfect sense for Hooper to prepare a set of legal papers never intended to be filed with any Court; the California client would receive a forged Decree of Adoption and have no reason to question further; and any rare inquiries made from Tennessee regarding the adoption would find nothing at the Court and attribute most likely to filing errors. The Department of Social Services, Adoptions Unit, maintained what the attorney firm and the Tennessee Children's Home Society sent them regarding the Tennessee and California actions. No independent contact between Social Services and the Superior Court in Santa Ana was ever made concerning the adoption.

Unless the Orange County Superior Court file A-22307 can be located, the hypothesis remains that Hooper & Miller received the adoption case from Georgia Tann, prepared an illegal adoption filing, forged clerk stamps and court signatures, and disseminated copies of same to the adoptive parents, Department of Social Services, and the TCHS as if they were genuine.

It is interjected that the evidentiary "Doctrine of the Fruit of the Poisoned Tree" applies in this scenario from the point the victim was removed from Wright's Clinic to Chattanooga under false "Color of Authority" and the paternal Mother's signature forged on the Surrender document. Nothing from that point in the case was legally binding or possible under the law. The Tennessee and California adoption proceedings are null and void, and of no force and effect.

On March 12, 2013, DNA testing results from AncestryDNA, LLC were received covering paternity, ethnicity, and background history. The test was conducted from samples provided by the victim and Elbert Griffith, brother to Arnold Lafayette Griffith resulting in a 99 percentile match of paternal relationship. The test also confirmed in satellite matches with other DNA submissions of record, a direct maternal relationship to the Bowman family by the Kilgore family lineage. The victim's biological parents were confirmed by DNA analysis as Flossie Bowman and Arnold Griffith. Testing ruled out Lenard Arnold Harris as a biological father.

Through the completion of the California adoption of the victim in 1953, the issue of a divorce between Bowman and Harris remained a sticking point to clear the adoption for completion. Repeated requests were made from the Tennessee Department of Social Welfare and the California Department of Social Services to verify her divorce from Harris. Contradictory reports were received from the Marion County Circuit Court Clerk Wallace Brown in Jasper, and Juvenile Court Judge Camille McGee Kelley who was assigned by Tann to quell the issue. Clerk Brown reported that no record of divorce was found. Judge Kelley reported that no divorce was "completed". So it is probable that an action for dissolution of the marriage was begun in Marion County by Flossie Bowman using attorney McClarney as Bowman declared. It was true in 1949 that court clerk procedures for receiving new filings were logged in a civil, criminal, or probate index officially documenting receipt of the case filing, thereto any filing caused by Bowman would be of record whether completed or not. It is highly possible and extremely easy for Judge Kelley to have any record of a filed case to just 'disappear'; the case file discarded or just 'pulled' and not returned and entry in the index blotted out as a simple miss-entry.

The issue of divorce was paramount to the planned adoption scheme. Without a dissolution of record, Harris and Bowman remained married, requiring Harris to be named as the "legal" father. Mr. Harris had absolutely no clue as to Flossie's pregnancy, giving birth, or the subsequent adoption proceedings and no attempts were ever conducted to locate Harris or Griffith. In the well-laid plans of Tann and her conspirators, any 'accidental' contact with Harris by aggravated adoptive parents or invasive investigators would be met with blank confusion.

The deception was complete. Tann knew with the assistance of Hooper & Miller out in California, the state would just rubber stamp what Tennessee sent them and finish the adoption. In March 1953 James Arnold Bowman officially became Donald Walter Boehner.

No one ever asked what ever happened to Baby James.

A number of habeas corpus and probate cases have been brought against the Tann estate, and the Tennessee Children's Home Society, and none resulted in any financial reimbursement or return of stolen children to their natural parents. Virtually all the principals involved in 1949 are now deceased, taking to their grave the secrets and deceptions involving thousands of Tennessee children. Some children will never find their natural parents, and in turn, most parents who lost their children have passed away before finding they survived. Some of us did survive to find our families.

It is not enough to know of the atrocities committed by the TCHS and how closely their predetermined acts align to this specific case, but evidence admissible in a court of law beyond mere speculation. Further evidence must be gathered from social services entities, a Questioned Document Examiner must be retained to give a professional determination upon the various signatures of Flossie Bowman, and additional attempts to locate the elusive California adoption file must be made. Upon the supposition that the Surrender form is the basis for all adoptions proceedings thereafter, a determination that the signature is a forgery would nullify the remaining actions, allowing the revocation of court Orders granted in the Tennessee and California cases. The task of finding a willing lawyer to handle such a case in Tennessee would be a monumental undertaking unless their case was prepared for them in advance; a Southern California lawyer to handle that location hearing would be easier to find under their more liberal view of justice. Attempting to raise a criminal prosecution directed against the State of Tennessee for violations under gross negligence of the mother and victim's civil rights would be a very difficult and costly action to pursue.

Findings & Recommendations ~

The summary findings of the investigation into the abduction, and subsequent black market sale-for-profit adoption of James Arnold Bowman by the Tennessee Children's Home Society, is as follows:

- On or about May 18, 1949 the victim was identified as a perspective adoptee by Miss Margaret Hall and Mary Hawkins Wright;
- Between September 15th and the 30th, 1949 the victim was taken from the Mother's care while under control of Wright's Clinic, Marion County, in Jasper. During this time, Flossie was told the victim had died and that Wright's Clinic would take care of the remains;
- On December 8, 1949, named conspirators gathered at Wright's Clinic to forge the Surrender form necessary to further perpetuate

illegal adoption actions in Tennessee and California. A replica of Miss Bowman's signature was traced in pencil and then tracing the signature in fountain pen ink over the pencil trace.

- The forged signature on the Surrender form renders both State adoptions null, void, and of no force and effect, subject to revocation and restoration of birth status of the victim.

The conclusion advocates the revocation of both State adoption filings and the birth certificates created thereon; the restoration of the victim's birth name; and new Tennessee birth certificate created in the victim's birth name.

CHAPTER 7

CLOSING STATEMENTS

How does one process the events portrayed through these pages beginning with an accidental disclosure of adoption in 1957, and ending with an accidental disclosure of my adoption details in 2008. For some, the fact of being adopted at all can be a traumatic event; tossing in the illegal and immoral action of the Tennessee Children's Home Society, being stolen after birth and advertised as deceased and adopted out to California parents, is a whole lot to consume and process. It was not until I found my Bowman and Griffith families that a majority of the missing pieces of this 65 year old case began to fill in. It is difficult to read and receive information describing your natural mother as an alcoholic and a prostitute known and favored in the community as Mary Hawkins Wright described in her case narrative. Flossie's history was carefully and kindly represented by the Bowman family during our reunion of 2011, but as customary in most cases, actions speak louder than words. Flossie loved to drink and that was her love and passion which cost the loving family she could have had, and as 'birds of a feather' Arnold Griffith was in the same frame of mind. Their drinking and partying took center stage over their daughter Linda, and again with their son Eddie, who both at early ages were taken in by my Aunt Oma Griffith to raise them into adulthood. What they did not have was the intention or desire to surrender a child for adoption, as stated blatantly by Flossie in her May 20th letter to the TCHS. The couple lived their lives as they saw fit, enjoining their carefree lifestyle interjected with occasional family contacts or events, but not forming the normal family love and relationships most of us enjoy. Their life was a sad affair riddled by poverty, alcohol, domestic fights, and mutual separation for weeks or months at a time, but in all consideration, married in 1951 and remained together until Arnold's death in 1978. My brother Eddie had the hardest time growing up. Marked also by alcoholism and drug abuse, Eddie struggled with health problems, unemployment, and later disabilities due to his lifestyle which would eventually claim his life in 2011. In his later years, Eddie was baptized in the Spirit by his own son, the Reverend Ed Griffith, Jr. of Whitwell, Tennessee.

I cannot come to an understanding why my adoptive parents decided to keep my adoption details secret into my adulthood. Possibly they believed with my legal background and training I would surely find the secrets they didn't want me to know surrounding the TCHS. They obviously knew there were problems with the Tennessee adoption, especially after being notified of same by Tennessee Social Services as early as 1950. They could only assume that any possible inquiry would affect the adoption, possibly resulting in my untimely return to Tennessee. Whatever the reasons perceived, their misguided concerns cost me the opportunity of meeting my natural mother before her death in 1993, and the ability to receive a first-hand account of what exactly transpired in 1949. The handwritten instruction by my adopted mother on the envelope containing my Decree of Adoption read, "Not to be opened until after our deaths" explained it all; they were not prepared or would they ever be placed in a situation to answer questions concerning my adoption. They would never ask what ever happened to Baby James . . . they were afraid of the answers.

Finis

Exhibit List

Fig. 1: Certified Live Birth Certificate (Handwritten) #141-49-28302. June 13, 1949

Fig. 2: History Sheet prepared by Margaret Hall. December 8, 1949

Fig. 3: Decree of Adoption, Orange Co Superior Court, California #A-22307. March 4, 1953

Fig. 4: Typed letter, Margaret Hall to Flossie Bowman. May 16, 1949

Fig. 5: Handwritten in pencil letter, Flossie Bowman to Margaret Hall. May 20, 1949

Fig. 6: Typed letter, Margaret Hall to Mary Hawkins-Wright. May 25, 1949

Fig. 7: Case History prepared by Margaret Hall. December 8, 1949

Fig. 8: Certificate of Live Birth, TN state form, #141-49-85202. Created March 3, 1953. (6/8/49)

Fig. 9: Typed letter, Georgia Tann to Walt & Sidonia Boehner. September 30, 1949

Fig. 10: Typed letter, Margret Hall to Flossie Bowman. October 24, 1949

Fig. 11: Request For New Birth Certificate, TCHS form. March 12, 1952

Fig. 12: Handwritten letter, from Flossie Bowman to Margaret Hall. October 31, 1949

Fig. 13: Typed letter, Margaret Hall to Flossie Bowman. November 13, 1949

Fig. 14: Typed letter, Margaret Hall to Flossie Bowman. December 2, 1949

Fig. 15: Handwritten letter, Flossie Bowman to Margaret Hall. December 7, 1949

Fig. 16: Surrender For Adoption, TCHS form. December 8, 1949

Fig. 17: Signature Comparison Page. May 21, 2009

Fig. 18: Child's Own Family History prepared by Margaret Hall. December 26, 1949

Fig. 19: Examination and Recommendations Record, TCHS Memphis. December 9-13, 1949

Fig. 20: Typed letter. Margaret Hall (TCHS) to Mamie Lou Hall, Dir, Dept of Public Welfare, 12/12/49

Fig. 21: Record of Placement prepared by Margaret Hall. December 14, 1949

Fig. 22: Typed letter, CA Dept of Social Welfare to Vallie S. Miller, DSW Nashville. February 26, 1952

Fig. 23: Typed letter, Mamie Lou Hall (DSW) to Margaret Hall (TCHS). December 22, 1949

Fig. 24: Typed letter, Doris June Vinton (DSW Marion Co) to Vallie S. Miller Nashville. May 13, 1952

Fig. 25: Typed letter, JO McMahon, Comm DSW Nashville to to Walt & Sidonia Boehner. July 12, 1951

Fig. 26: Application For For Confidential Verification of Birth, Vallie Miller to Vital Statistics. 7/26/51

Fig. 27: Civil action, Surrender hearing, TCHS v. Harris and Bowman, #103-605. Date unknown

Fig. 28: Certificate of Relinquishment, TCHS. September 15, 1952

Fig. 29: Order For Adoption, Orange Co Superior Court, #A-22307. March 4, 1953

Fig. 30: Typed letter, Christine Reynolds (DSW Nashville) to Ralph Goss (DRW Los Angeles). 2/16/53

Fig. 31: Typed letter, Helen Chandler (DSW Los Angeles) to Christine Reynolds Nashville. 3/20/53

Fig. 32: Photo, Wright's Clinic, Jasper, TN, 2011, D. Boehner

Fig. 33: Photo, Georgia Tann, Wikipedia internet source

Fig. 34: Photo, Judge Camille Kelley, Wikipedia internet source

Fig. 35: Photo, TCHS orphanage and Georgia Tann's home, Wikipedia internet source

Fig. 36: Photo, TCHS Advertising, Wikipedia internet source

Fig. 37: Photo, Georgia Tann and Baby Lucy, Wikipedia internet source

Fig. 38: Photo, Don Boehner, 7 years old, D. Boehner

Fig. 39: Photo, Don Boehner, Army induction 1968, D. Boehner

Fig. 40: Photo, Don Boehner, 1951 – Cover Photo, D. Boehner

Fig.41: Photo, Don Boehner, 2008 – Book Flap Photo, D. Boehner

/////

Certificate of Live Birth

141 - 49 - 28302

James Arnold Bowman

Male.

born may 8, 1949

Marion Co., Jasper, Tenn   mother: Residence
        Wright Hospital   Whitwell, Tenn.

Father.

. . . . .

Mother.

Flossie Louise Bowman   white.

1 other child living.

Whitwell, Tenn.

Art. by Steven Bryan.
        Jasper, Tenn.   June 13, 1949.

Reg. Dist # 581

Fig. 1 Certificate of Live Birth May 8, 1949

Number of Record	Age	Sex	HISTORY SHEET	Date Received			
7702	inf	male		12-8-49			

Name of Child	Place of Birth	Month	Day	Year
James Arnold Bowman	Wright Hospital, Jasper, Tenn.	5	8	49

N hty	Church Relationship	Physical Condition
American-born	unknown	

Mental Condition	Where Taken From
infant	Wright Hospital, Jasper, Tenn.

By Whom	Cause for Release to T. C. H. Society
Miss Margaret Hall	Born out of wedlock-unable to provide

Case Reported by	Address	How Reported	Date

How Released Surrender signed by mother

Is Child Illegitimate?	Half Orphan	Full Orphan	Examining Physician
yes			

Above Information Secured by Miss Margaret Hall

PARENTS AND RELATIVES

Name of Father	Address	Last Heard From at	Date
Arnold Griffeth	U.S. Army, Ft. Jackson, S.C.		

Name of Mother	Address	Last Heard From at	Date
Flossie Louise Bowman	Whitwell, Tenn.		

Age of Father	Living	Nationality	Place of Birth	Church Relationship
24	yes	American born		unknown

Age of Mother	Living	Nationality	Place of Birth	Church Relationship
24	yes	American born		Unknown

Occupation of Father	Name of Employer	Address of Employer	Financial Condition
U.S. Army			

Occupation of Mother	Name of Employer	Address of Employer	Financial Condition
Unknown			

Physical Condition of Father	Mental Condition of Father	Married Before	Divorced	Deserter	General Charact

Physical Condition of Mother	Mental Condition of Mother	Married Before	Divorced	Deserter	General Charact

Does Father Drink?	Use Any Drugs?	What Kind?	Informant	Address

Does Mother Drink?	Use Any Drugs?	What Kind?	Informant	Address

Names of Other Children	Sex	Age	Married	Present Address

Remarks About Other Children

Names of Relatives	Addresses of Relatives	Remarks

Other References	Addresses	Remarks

Fig. 2 History Sheet #1 12/8/49

FILED
MAR 4 - 1953
SMITH
COUNTY CLERK
By _____ Deputy

IN THE SUPERIOR COURT OF THE STATE OF CALIFORNIA

IN AND FOR THE COUNTY OF ORANGE

IN THE MATTER OF THE ADOPTION)   No. A-22307

OF)   <u>DECREE OF ADOPTION</u>

JAMES ARNOLD BOWMAN, a Minor)

WALTER A. BOEHNER and SIDONIA C. BOEHNER, having presented their petition praying for approval of their adoption of
the above named minor child, and the said matter coming on regu-
larly to be heard, GEORGE A. HOOPER appearing as attorney for
the petitioners, and there appearing before the Court the petitioners and the above named minor child who were examined by
the Court, each separately, from which examination it is found
that the petitioners are husband and wife, and are residents of
the County of Orange, State of California.

That on the 5th day of May, 1949, the above named chi
was born in the City of Jasper, County of Marion, State of Tenn
see, unto FLOSSIE LOUISE BOWMAN FARRIS, wife of LEONARD A. FARR

That heretofore a Court of competent jurisdiction in
the State of Tennessee declared said child free from the custod
of said parents and deprived said parents of the custody of sai
child; that the TENNESSEE CHILDREN'S HOME SOCIETY, an incorpora

Fig. 3 Decree of Adoption – CA 3/5/53

May 16, 1949

Miss Flossie Bowman
c/o Mrs. Josie Van Hoosier
Whitwell,
Tennessee

Dear Miss Bowman:

A few days ago when I happened to be visiting at Wright's Clinic
in Jasper, Miss Wright mentioned to me that you might be interested
in adoptive service for your baby. She was not sure just what
arrangement you planned to make for it when it is ready to leave
the hospital.

Our Society specializes in adoptive service. We find suitable homes
for children who need adoption and supervise the home one year before
legal adoption takes place.

If you are interested in our service I shall be glad to talk with you
about it. Through Miss Wright I obtained directions to your home but
she was not sure that she planned to stay there very long. If I can
help you please let me know where I can find you. I am enclosing a
self-addressed stamped enveloped for your reply.

Yours very truly,

(Miss) Margaret Hall
Field Secretary

TCHS

Fig. 4 Hall Letter 5/16/49

Dear Friend   May 20. 49
I am not intersted in
giving my baby away
and I dident say I was
going to give it away
I have a home for
both of them. with me
some people was trying
to get me to give
the baby away.
I wouldent give one of
my Children away for
nothing in the world.
that was some one
elses idea. not mine
thank you for offering
to help me. but I dont
need that kind of help.
                    Miss Bouman

Fig. 5 Flossie Letter 5/20/49

May 25, 1949

Miss Mary Hawkins Wright   Re: Miss Flossie Bowman
Wright's Hospital   Whitwell, Tennessee
Jasper, Tennessee

Dear Miss Wright:

Under date of May 20 I had a letter from the above named mother.
She stated that she was not interested in giving up her baby. "I
wouldent give one of my children away for nothing in the world.
Thank you for offering to help me. but I dont need that kind of
help," she says in her letter. She goes on to say that she has
a home for both of her children with her.

You have no doubt heard from her yourself by now. She is probably
one of those persons who look upon adoption as "sinful".

I cannot begin to tell you how much we appreciate your splendid
cooperation. I have thought so many times of what a marvelous
contribution you are making to your community. I just do not
see how you do it all. One recognizes immediately, however, that
you love your work and I suppose it is because of this that you
are able to do so much.

I wish you all the success in the world and think that your community
is mighty lucky to have a person like you in it.

                                Sincerely,

                                Margaret Hall
                                Field Secretary

MH/bm

Fig. 6 Hall Letter 5/25/49

Pl. Easter C.
12/14/49

Baby Boy Bowman
B.D. 5/8/49.

Birth date: May 8, 1949
Birth weight - premature- 3 lbs.
Present weight: 13 lbs. 2 oz.

BABY- Baby was premature, weighed only three pounds at birth but has developed normally in every way. Kahn was negative, Wasserman and smear on mother negative. Has not had any childhood diseases or immunizations.

MOTHER- 22 years of age, American born, of English-Irish extraction. High school education, had blue-gray eyes, medium brown hair, about 5 ft. 2 in. tall, weight 120 pounds. Protestant in religion. Considered very pretty and intelligent.

FATHER- 23 years of age, American born, of German-Scotch and English extraction. Had light brown eyes, medium brown hair. High school education, Lutheran in religion. Was about 5 ft. 11 in. tall, weight about 185 lbs.

No inheritable diseases on either side of the families and both maternal and paternal families well respected in their own communities

Fig. 7 Case History #2 12/14/49

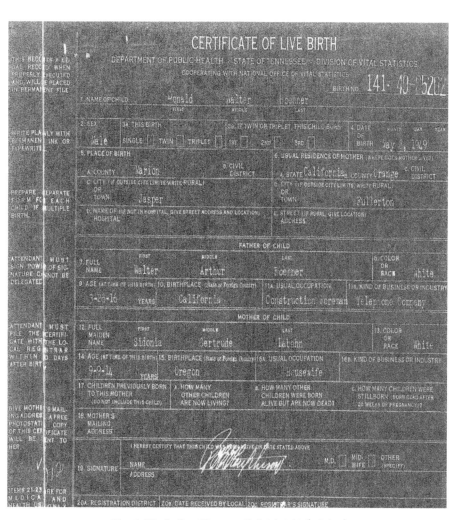

Fig. 8 Birth Certificate—CA 3/1953 (6/8/49)

Sept. 30, 1949

Mr. and Mrs. Walter A. Boehner
505 So. Sunset Blvd.,
Temple City, California

My Dear Mr. and Mrs. Boehner:

This letter is written to advise you that your home has definitely been accepted for the placement of a child.

You will doubtless recall that Mrs. Walton explained to you that due to the many applications already on file and approved, it may be from six months to a year after the home had been visited and approved before a placement could be made. However, in some instances we are able to make a placement much sooner than we had expected and you may rest assured that just as soon as the proper child is available, we will get in touch with you.

Due to congested traveling conditions, it is my advice that you have one of our trained workers bring the child to you. Traveling, at best, is difficult, even for a trained worker, and this suggestion is made for this reason.

Sincerely yours,

Georgia Tann
Asst. State Superintendent

GT-HW   TENNESSEE CHILDREN'S HOME SOCIETY

Fig. 9 Tann Letter 9/30/49

December 2nd, 1949

Miss Flossie Bowman
Whitewell,
Tennessee

Dear Flossie:

I received you letter this morning. It will be impossible for me to
meet you on December 5th. Will Thursday, December 8th, be all right?
I can meet you in Whitwellat the post office at 1:00, as you suggest-
ed. The only reason why I think it will be better to meet in Jasper
is that you will have to sign papers before a Notary Public and I have
a feeling that you would not like for anyone in Whitwell to know what
you are doing. If you do not object to this it will be all right with
me. I thought it could be done in Jasper more privately. Think it
over again and let me know right away where I sould met you and if Thursday, December 8th at 1:00 is all right. If you decide to come to Jasper
I can meet you at Wright's Hospital.

                              Yours very truly,

                              (Miss) Margaret Hall
                              Field Secretary

MJH:bm

Fig. 10 Hall Letter 10/24/49

REQUEST FOR A NEW CERTIFICATE OF BIRTH BY ADOPTION

TO: DIVISION OF VITAL STATISTICS
TENNESSEE DEPARTMENT OF PUBLIC HEALTH
NASHVILLE, TENNESSEE

DATE __September 12, 1952__

PLEASE PREPARE A NEW CERTIFICATE OF BIRTH FOR THIS CHILD. FULL INFORMATION REQUIRED FOR THE CERTIFICATE IS GIVEN BELOW BY THE ADOPTIVE PARENTS:

FULL NAME OF CHILD __DONALD__ __WALTER__ __BOEHNER__
FIRST · MIDDLE · LAST

DATE OF BIRTH __May__ __8__ __1949__
MO. · DAY · YEAR

FATHER	MOTHER
FULL NAME __WALTER__ __ARTHUR__ __BOEHNER__ FIRST · MIDDLE · LAST	Maiden FULL NAME __SIDONIA__ __GERTRUDE__ __LABAHN__ FIRST · MIDDLE · LAST
COLOR OR RACE __WHITE__	COLOR OR RACE __WHITE__
DATE OF BIRTH __March 26__ __1916__ MO. · DAY · YEAR	DATE OF BIRTH __September__ __9__ __1914__ MO. · DAY · YEAR
BIRTHPLACE __California__ STATE OR FOREIGN COUNTRY	BIRTHPLACE __Oregon__ STATE OR FOREIGN COUNTRY
USUAL OCCUPATION __Construction Foreman__	USUAL OCCUPATION __Housewife__
KIND OF INDUSTRY OR BUSINESS __Telephone Company__	KIND OF INDUSTRY OR BUSINESS

WE, THE ABOVE-NAMED PARENTS, HEREBY CERTIFY THAT THE INFORMATION GIVEN HEREIN IS CORRECT TO THE BEST OF OUR KNOWLEDGE AND BELIEF.

SIGNATURES:

FATHER _Walter A Boehner_

MOTHER _Sidonia G. Labahn Boehner_

MAILING ADDRESS: __500 El Camino Drive__ __Fullerton__ __California__
STREET AND NUMBER · CITY · STATE

Fig. 11 Request For New Certificate of Birth (CA) 9/12/52

Fig. 12 Flossie Letter 10/24/49

November 3rd, 1949

Miss Flossie Bowman
Whitwell,
Tennessee

Dear Flossie:

I received your letter this morning. I will meet you at
Miss Wright's on November 15th, 1949, at 1:00 P.M.

Thank you very much.

Yours very truly,

(Miss) Margaret Hall
Field Secretary

MJH:bm

Fig. 13 Hall Letter 11/3/49

December 2nd, 1949

Miss Flossie Bowman
Whitewell,
Tennessee

Dear Flossie:

I received your letter this morning. It will be impossible for me to
meet you on December 5th. Will Thursday, December 8th, be all right?
I can meet you in Whitewell at the post office at 1:00, as you suggest-
ed. The only reason why I think it will be better to meet in Jasper
is that you will have to sign papers before a Notary Public and I have
a feeling that you would not like for anyone in Whitewell to know what
you are doing. If you do not object to this it will be all right with
me. I thought it could be done in Jasper more privately. Think it
over again and let me know right away where I could met you and if Thursday, December 8th at 1:00 is all right. If you decide to come to Jasper
I can meet you at Wright's Hospital.

Yours very truly,

(Miss) Margaret Hall
Field Secretary

MJH:bm

Fig. 14 Hall Letter 12/2/49

Dec. 7, 1949
Whitewell, Tenn

Miss Margaret Hall

Dear Miss Hall
           In answer to your
letter received yesterday
I will meet you in
person at Miss Wright
Thursday Dec. 8th at
one O. Clock.

                    Yours Truly
                    Flossie Brewer

Fig. 15 Flossie Letter 12/7/49

Parent's or Guardian's

SURRENDER

TO

Tennessee Children's Home Society

MRS. FANNIE B. ELROD, Supt.
901 Acklen Avenue
NASHVILLE, TENN.

HELP A CHILD FIND A HOME IS OUR MOTTO

Register No. of Child... **7702**

Name... James Arnold Bowman

Sex... Male... Color... White

Date of Birth... 5-8-49

Place of Birth... Wright Hospital
Jasper, Tenn.

Date of Release to Society... 12-5-49

With Whom Placed...

When Placed...

Marion Co.

PARENTS OF CHILD

Father... Arnold Griffeth

Residence... US Army, Ft. Jackson, S.C.

Mother... Flossie Louise Bowman

Residence... Whitwell, Tenn.

Nationality of Father... American Born

Occupation of Father... U.S. Army

Member of What Church... Unknown

Character of Father...... Age... 24

Nationality of Mother... American Born

Occupation of Mother... Unknown

Member of What Church... Unknown

Character of Mother...... Age... 24

No. of Children in Family... 1

Cause of Child's Dependency... born out of
... wedlock.

WHERE WAS CHILD FOUND?

County... Marion... City... Jasper

No... Wright Hospital... Street...

Poorhouse—Yes or No...

Elsewhere...

MEDICAL EXAMINATION

Of...

Is the Child:

Healthy?...

Robust?...

Deformed?...... Crippled?...

Diseased?...... If so, how?...

Is disease chronic, incurable, or contagious?...

Which?...

Is child ruptured?...

If so, how seriously?...

Is child feeble-minded?...

Epileptic?...

Do you know of any bad physical heredity?...

What?...

Is the child, in your judgment, fit to be placed in a f
home?...

Remarks...

Signed...... 19

P. O. Address...... M.

Fig. 16 Surrender Form – Page 1 12/8/49

Tennessee Children's Home Society

For and in consideration of certain undertakings of The Tennessee Children's Home Society, and especially that of finding a suitable home where the said child herein named may be properly provided for, and for other good and valuable considerations, the undersigned, being the { ~~Father~~ Mother ~~Guardian~~ } of a certain MALE child named JAMES HAROLD BOWMAN, born (date) MAY 8, 1949

In Wedlock   Out of Wedlock ✓   hereby give S and surrender S the said child to said Society and authorize S said Society to keep and care for said child until it can find for said child such suitable family home, and to put said child in such home, and to make and enter into suitable terms of agreement with the person taking the same.

And the undersigned hereby also give S and grant S to the person taking said child from the said Society the same parental control and authority that the undersigned would have had if SHE had retained said child and authorize S the legal adoption of said child by the persons with whom it may be placed by said Society.

And the undersigned further agree S to neither seek to discover said child's home, attempt its removal therefrom, either physically or by taking any proceeding tending to that end, nor in any way to molest the family in which HE may be placed or the persons interested.

And the undersigned also authorize S The Tennessee Children's Home Society, by its attorney or agent, to appear in any proceeding for its legal adoption and consent to its adoption.

The undersigned recognize S MRS. PANWIE D. ELIROD

as the superintendent and agent of said Society, and authorize S HER or HER successor in office to act for said Society.

The undersigned further agree that, if said child should prove to be mentally or physically unfit for placement, it may be returned to its county, or to the custodian whose name or names are signed hereto.

IN WITNESS WHEREOF, the undersigned hereunto set HER hand and seal, this 8th day of December A. D. 19 49

Florsie Louise Bowman (Seal.)

....(Seal.)

...., Guardian.

WITNESS:

Howard G. Swofford

MARION

~~HAMILTON~~ County, } SS.

State of Tennessee. }

Witness: Mary Hamlain Wright

I hereby certify that this day appeared before me, the undersigned, a Notary Public in and for said County and State, Florsie Louise Bowman, to me personally known to be the identical person whose name is signed to the foregoing instrument as MOTHER of the child therein named, and acknowledged the instrument to be HER voluntary act and deed for the uses and purposes therein named.

Fig. 16—Page 2 12/8/49

Donald Walter Boehner

Case # A-22307

Request For Release of Adoption Records and Order

EXHIBIT C

SIGNATURE COMPARISONS

MAY 20, 1949: *Miss Bowman*

DECEMBER 7, 1949: *Flossie Bowman*

DECEMBER 8, 1949: *Flossie Louise Bowman*

5/20/1949: Personal letter handwritten by Flossie Louise Bowman, pencil on lined tablet paper.

12/7/1949: Represented as a personal letter from Flossie Bowman the day before Adoptee's surrender form was executed at Wright's Clinic in Jasper, TN:

12/8/1949: TCHS agency form, Parent's or Guardian's Surrender to Tennessee Children's Home Society. Authorizes the TCHS to take physical possession of Adoptee and used as the basis and authority for all other adoptive actions in TN and CA. A pencil line is noted behind the ink signature.

/////

/////

/////

Fig. 17 Signature Comparison 2014

CHILD'S OWN FAMILY

Child's Name James Arnold Bowman Birthdate 5-8-49 Birthplace Wright Hospital, Jasper, Ten

Mother's Name Flossie Louise Bowman Age 24 Address Whitwell, Tennessee

Father's Name Arnold Griffeth Age 24 Address U.S. Army, Ft. Jackson, South Carolina

Surrendered 12-8-49 Worker Margaret Hall

Referral: This baby was born prematurely and at the time of birth the mother talked with Miss
Mary Hawkins Wright, RN, Wright Hospital, Jasper, Tennessee, about release for
adoption. Knowing the baby was born out of wedlock, that the mother had another child also
born out of wedlock, and the type of life she was living Miss Wright encouraged the mother to
consider adoption. Miss Wright was of the opinion that this premature baby would not have
received proper care if the mother kept it. When the mother left the hospital the baby remain
ed in an incubator until it weighed around 6 lbs. Miss Wright asked me to get in touch with
the mother regarding adoption. I wrote the mother a letter offering her our service. She replied that she was not interested in releasing her child for adoption (the letter was not writt
in the mother's handwriting we later learned).

When the mother took the baby from the hospital she apparently had no plan except for her
sister to look after it. Miss Wright felt that it was the sister who was influncing Flossie
to keep the baby. In September Flossie returned the baby to Wright's Hospital. Dr. McMillian
found it to be undernourished and suffering with diarrhea. He ordered the mother to take it
to Children's Hospital in Chattanooga. It was admitted with a diagnosis of "infectious diarrh
Again Miss W. encouraged the mother to release the baby but she refused to do it.

Around November 15th Flossie called Miss Wright and said the baby was sick again, that she did
not have money to buy milk with and that the baby's father was in the guardhouse and could no
longer send her money. She said she had decided to release the baby and would like to talk
with me about plans. On 11-10-49 she took the baby to Miss W. with the understanding that I
would accept custody and start adoption plans. When Miss W. advised that the baby was in her
hospital I said I would pay her board if she would care for the baby until I could get the
mother to sign a release. I did not want to move the baby from Marion County until the mother
had signed the release. I knew that she was not dependable and uncooperative (see correspondence in file).

On 12-8-49 I met Flossie at Wright's Hospital. Our appointment was for 1:00 P.M. An hour
later, however, she called from Whitwell saying that she would get a taxi and come right over.
When she arrived, around 3:00 PM, her and 2 men were in the car with her. She had them to
wait outside for her. I explained that I needed certain information and that the interview
and the signing of the release would take some time. She said it would be all right for them
to wait for her. I interviewed her in Miss Wright's bedroom. She was vague and not too co-
operative in giving information.

The Mother: Flossie Louise Bowman was born Janurary 15th, 1929, at Whitwell, Tenn., where sh
has lived all of her life. Her father Joe William Bowman, died in 1947, at the
age of 68. He was a miner and had to quit work at the age of 65 because of "spells". I asked
if they were epileptic seizures and she did not know. I described a seizure and she said yes
the spells he had were like that. She did not think however, that he had them until the last
few years of his life. She felt sure he could not work in the mines had he had them before.
He was married 3 times and Flossie was by his last marriage. His first wife and his second
wife died. Flossie's mother is Nancy (Kilgore) Mosier, age 46. She has remarried sincer her
husband's death

*(see letter attached regarding Mr. Bowman's health)

Fig. 18 Child's Own Family History #3—Page 1 12/26/49

Flossie says she has 1 whole sister and 3 whole brothers, 1 half-sister, and 5 half-brothers, all of whom live and work in the mines at Whitwell.

Flossie says she lives alone. During the War she worked at the Star Woolen Mill in South Pittsburgh, Tenn. Since then she has worked as a waitress. According to Miss Wright she is well-known in the community for her promiscuity. She worked at a "honky-tonk" at Sequatch. and is believed to have been prostituting. She completed the 5th grade. She is about 5'8" tall and weighs 125lbs. She has hazel eyes, light brown hair, high cheek bones and dimples on her cheeks. She might be pretty if it were not for her receding chin. She says that she has always been in good health and that there is no history of inheritable diseases in her family unless it could be the "spells" her father had.

When she was 16 years old she said she was married to Lenord Harris on June 25th, 1945, and that they were divorced in Marion County a short time later. Attorney McClarney handled the divorce. According to a letter from the Department of Public Welfare, Marion County, Jasper, Tenn., (see letter in file) there is no recording in Marion County of this divorce. Attorney McClarney advised that Flossie consulted him at one time about a divorce but did not carry through.

Flossie has a little girl, Linda Jane Griffith, born 12-47. She says the father of the baby is also the father of Linda Jane. We had understood from Miss Wright that Linda Jane lived with Flossie's sister. However, after she signed release she remarked she would go by the Welfare Department to tell them she had released the baby for adoption. She then explained that she was already receiving an ADC grant for Linda Jane and that the baby had been added to it. I told her that I would notify the Department and that she should speak with them also I went by the Department of Public Welfare to see Miss Mamie Lou Hall, the director, but she was not in. I later notified her by letter.

The Father: Flossie says Arnold Griffith, age 24, is the father of her baby. She says his home is at Griffith Creek, in Marion County. His mother has a store there. His father is dead and he has several brothers and sisters. He is believed to have attended high school He is blonde, about 5'9" tall and weighs 145 lbs. At the present he is in the guard house at Ft. Jackson, South Carolina. Flossie says he used to give her some financial help for both children until he got in the guardhouse. She does not know why he is being confined. Miss W stated that the only reason Flossie's family wanted her to keep the baby was in order to keep the father sending money. When they knew no money was forthcoming they consented to adoption

The Baby: James Arnold Bowman was born 5-8-49 at Wright's Hospital. Dr. McMillian delivered. The mother had no prenatal care and entered the hospital as an emergency. She had a negative Wasserman. The baby progressed satisfactorily and would probably have gotten along all right had he had the proper care. The infectious diaherrea in September set him back considerably. Miss Wright boarded him for us from November 18th to December 8th. She said she thought he was normal and that all he needed was a permanent home where he would get the proper care.

12-8-49: Transferred to Memphis Receiving Home for observation and placement.

MJH:bm
12-26-49

Fig. 18 Child's Own Family History #3 – Page 2 12/26/49

EXAMINATIONS AND RECOMMENDATIONS

Name of Child _Bowman James Arnold_ Sex _m_   Date of Birth _5 - 8_   19 _49_

Dates of Examinations _12/9/49_   _B. W. 3 -_

A____mplaint?____ _7 mo._   _12/12_

Menstrual History since last visit on adolescent girl_____

Height_____

Weight____ _996_ _12-14_

Temperature_____

Skin____ _Clear_

Scalp____ _ok_

Eyes____ _non conjed_   _Continuous_

Ears____

Nose____

Teeth____

Throat____

Adenoids____

Glands____

Thyroid____

Chest____

Heart____ _OK_

Lungs____ _OK_

Abdomen____

Se__dary Sex Characteristics____

Genitals____

Reflexes____

Extremities____

Feet____

Posture and Spine____

Nutrition____ _Good_

TESTS AND INOCULATIONS

Examining Physician _____ Dr. _____

Fig. 19 Exam and Recommendations – Page 1 12/9/49

James Arnold Bowman B. date 5.8.49 B. wt 3 —

| STOOLS | | FORMULA FEEDING | | | | | BREAST | | | | CLINICAL SYMPTOMS AND REMARKS | |
NO.	TYPE											
7	mo	Baby boy from Chattanooga										1
wt	12	9.4	—			Congested nose — Flenigan						2
12	10	8 oz	took all				good color	nose B				3
												4
												5
												6
												7
												8
												9
												10
												11
												12
												13
												14
												15
												16
												17
												18
												19
												20
												21
												22
												23
												24
												25

Fig. 19 Examination and Recommendations – Page 2 12/9/49

DOCTOR	NO.	NAME	AGE SEX	WEIGHT TODAY	WEIGHT YEST'DY	TEMP.	
12 - 9		Bowman	12¹⁴				1
8 oz Formula		10 - 2 Took	all at 10 J. M.				2
left 2 oz at 2		stool Good					3
2-9. 8 oz. took 1 oz. 6 PM very slowly				nose drops Hall			4
							5
12 - 9. 8 oz		Formula 4 oz all		1 stool			6
		nose drops		B oluz			7
12-9- Vi-Penta juice-cereal-Strained squash							8
							9
12-10. cereal took 1 oz. milk 6 PM				Hall			10
							11
12 - 11							12
		Vi penta juice					13
		cereal					14
12-11 cereal took 1 oz. milk 6 PM				Hall			15
12 - 11 8 oz. took 7 - 6 PM				1 stool Nurse			16
			6 P				17
12 - 12		8 oz milk took all					18
		8 oz milk left 10 c		4 oz			19
				B oluz			20
12 - 12		8 oz milk took 6 oz		Nurse			21
12-13 Vi-Penta Orange j. nosegtts			13¼				22
3 vii-10-Took 3 v Took 3/01 at 2 C. 7							23
12-13. cereal took 4 oz 9 - 6 PM				Hall			24
		19 remiss d to mr Walton 12-13-49 (8³⁰PM)					25

Fig. 19 Examination and Recommendations – Page 3 12/9/49

December 12th, 1949

Miss Mamie Lou Hall
County Director
Department of Public Welfare
Jasper, Tennessee

Re: James Arnold Bowman
      Born: May 8th, 1949
      Mother: Flossie Louise Bowman
               Whitwell, Tennessee

Dear Miss Hall:

I was sorry I missed seeing you when I was in Jasper on December 8th. I wanted to tell you that the above named child had been released to the Tennessee Children's Home Society for the purpose of adoption.

The mother was interested in placing this child for adoption at the time he was born. You no doubt know that he was born prematurely and required considerable attention. It seems that members of her family urged her to keep the child. When he became seriously ill and was admitted to T. C. Thompson Children's Hospital in September, she again considered release. Finally, on November 18th, we accepted custody of the child for a period of study and observation to determine adoptability and on December 8th arrangements for release were completed.

It was not however, until after we obtained final release that we learned this child had been included in an ADC grant. We felt sure you would like to have this information. The mother stated that she, too, would get in touch with you.

We wonder if your record contains verification of the mother's divorce from Lenor Harris and any history of epilepsy in the mother's family. We understand her father was subject "to spells" during the last few years of his life. We would appreciate any information along this line you might be able to give us.

Thank you very much.

                    Yours very truly,

                    (Miss) Margaret Hall, Field Secretary

Fig. 20 Hall Letter 12/12/49

NUMBER OF RECORD	RECORD OF PLACEMENT	DATE PLACED IN HOME:
7702		Dec. 1949 14

NAME OF CHILD	REMARKS
James Arnold Bowman	Guardianship, mother's surrender 12-8-49

PLACED WITH

Mr. and Mrs. Walter A. Boehner

CITY	RURAL ROUTE	COUNTY	STATE
~~Memphis~~ Fullerton	500 El Camino Drive	Shelby	~~Tenn.~~ California

TERMS OF PLACEMENT	LENGTH OF TIME ON TRIAL
adoption	one year

RECORD OF LEGAL ADOPTION

NAME OF FATHER AND MOTHER

Walter A. & Sidonia Glabahn Boehner

ADDRESS

05 South Sunset Blvd., Temple City, California : moved to 500 EL Camino Drive,Fullerton .Calif.

CHILD'S NEW NAME	PLACE OF ADOPTION
~~James Arnold Bowman~~ Donald Walter Boehner	

REMARKS

RECORD OF RETURN OF CHILD TO HOME

REGISTERED NO.	DATE OF RETURN	HOW RETURNED

CAUSE FOR RETURN

Fig. 21 Record of Placement (TCHS) 12/14/49

AREA OFFICES

LOS ANGELES OFFICE
MErcury 6411
MIRROR BUILDING
145 South Spring Street
12

SACRAMENTO OFFICE
GILbert 2-4711
924 9th Street
14

SAN FRANCISCO OFFICE
EXbrook 2-8751
GRAYSTONE BUILDING
948 Market Street
2

STATE HEADQU
SACRAMEN
GILbert 2-v
616 K Stre
14

Earl Warren
Governor

STATE OF CALIFORNIA

Department of Social Welfare

CHARLES I. SCHOTTLAND
DIRECTOR

FEB 28 1952

Los Angeles
February 26, 1952

ADDRESS REPLY TO:

145 South Spring Street
Los Angeles 12

Mrs. Vallie S. Miller
Supervisor of Child Welfare
Department of Public Welfare
State Office Building
Nashville 3, Tennessee

Dear Mrs. Miller:

Adoption of James Arnold Bowman
By Mr. and Mrs. Walter A. Boehner
O of 3 B

We are glad to send you our report on Mr. and Mrs. Boehner of
Fullerton, California, who wish to adopt James Arnold Bowman, now known as
Donald Walter.

We first interviewed the family in their home in Temple City on
October 5, 1951, at which time both adoptive parents and Donald were present.
We made a subsequent visit on December 19, when Mrs. Boehner and the boy
only were present.

Donald, aged approximately two and a half, is a nice-looking boy,
rather tall for his age, with blue eyes, blond hair, and fair complexion.
According to a medical report of October 23, 1951, his height was three
feet and his weight thirty pounds. His right eye seems to turn slightly in,
and Mrs. Boehner said he had a scar on his left leg and asked whether we
knew the reason for it, but we had no information. While observing the boy,
we noticed that he was "drooling" quite a bit. Mrs. Boehner explained to
us that Donald had a great deal of saliva continuously dripping out of his
mouth when he first came to their home but that it had improved. She had
even called their family physician's attention to it, but he advised her
not to worry.

Information regarding Donald's maternal grandfather having had a
history of convulsions was discussed with Mr. and Mrs. Boehner. It was sug-
gested to them to have an electro-encephalogram taken on the boy, but both
Mr. and Mrs. Boehner appeared somewhat resistant to this suggestion, and we
advised them to discuss it with their family physician. As a result we
received a medical report on Donald with the following comment: "I do not
regard the epileptic history of any significance in this case for it is
unrelated to anything hereditary, nor are any further tests necessary from
such definite history." On October 18, 1951, Donald had an X-ray of the

Fig. 22 DSW Letter (CA)—Page 1 2/26/52

chest and findings were negative.

On my follow-up visit on December 19, 1951, I was able to observe Donald more. He named all the animals and other items in his picture book, was quite amenable to Mrs. Boehner's request to go and play for a short time in his own room. At the same time he asked for extra attention, and while being in the same room he kept on talking to Mrs. Boehner when she was talking to the agent, throwing toys on the floor, and banged the door when she was gone. Because of the health history of Donald's maternal grandfather and of Donald's drooling, we asked for a psychometric test on him. This was done, and a report sent to us by Dr. O'Neil, child psychologist, gives the following information: "Chronological Age: 2 years, 7 months; Mental Age: 2 years, 9 months; I. Q. 110-112. The basal age was attained at 2 years, 6 months, with two months on the three-year level, and one month on the three-year, six-month level. The child is quite hyperactive, jumping from one thing to another, and it was difficult to hold his attention. My impression is that this child is brighter than the test results indicate. However, he is placed in the bright-normal group." Mr. and Mrs. Boehner were well-impressed with the test and they spoke favorably of this experience.

The family have recently purchased a new home at 500 El Camino Drive, Fullerton, and they are moving to this home in the near future. They are planning to sell their present home.

Both Mr. and Mrs. Boehner are very fond of Donald and there appears to be an excellent relationship between them and the boy. References have been favorable. Medical reports have disclosed no adverse health condition. Mr. Boehner continues to be employed by the Pacific Telephone and Telegraph Company as their construction foreman. In addition to his employment, they own an unencumbered avocado ranch in Orange County, and they stated that they derive approximately $380 a year income from it.

We would feel satisfied to make a favorable recommendation on this adoption, it appearing that the child is a proper subject for adoption and the home of the adoptive parents is suitable, if a Certificate of Relinquishment is received from your office. (Consent and Agreement).

Very truly yours,

RALPH L. GOFF, Area Deputy

By *[signature]*

Mrs. Natalia L. Tschekaloff
Adoptions Worker

Fig. 22 DSW Letter (CA) – Page 2 2/26/52

STATE OF TENNESSEE

DEPARTMENT OF PUBLIC WELFARE

Marion County
Jasper, Tennessee
December 22, 1949

. O. McMAHAN
COMMISSIONER

Miss Margaret Hall
Field Secretary
Tennessee Children's Home Society
1323 Hamilton National Bank Building
Chattanooga, Tennessee

Re: James Arnold Bowman
Born: 5-6-49
Mother: Flossie Louise Bowman
Whitwell, Tennessee

Dear Miss Hall:

Mr. Joe Bowman, father of Flossie, was known to this agency in as much as he drew assistance for two minor children. There was no indication of epilepsy shown in our case history. According to our medical statement, dated 10-30-46, his condition was diagnosed as hardening of the arteries. Mr. Bowman claimed to have had a paralytic stroke. In 1947 he was admitted to a hospital after suffering a stroke. Following this stroke we were told that he had convulsions. His death occurred 11-23-47.

Flossie was of the opinion that she was divorced from her husband but, according to the Circuit Court Clerk of Marion County, this divorce has not been granted.

If we can be of further assistance please advise.

Very truly yours,

(Miss) Mamie Lou Hall
County Director

By
(Mrs.) Lena H. Simpson
Welfare Worker

LHS:ms

Fig. 23 Hall Letter (TDPW) 12/22/49

P
I

Department of Public Welfare
Marion County
Jasper, Tennessee
May 13, 1952

Vallie S. Miller, Director
Division of Field Service Consultants
Department of Public Welfare
204 State Office Building
Nashville, 3, Tennessee

Re: James Arnold Bowman, born 5-9-49
Mother: Flossie Louise Bowman,
Whitwell, Tennessee

Dear Mrs. Miller:

Mrs. McGavock has given to us your letter of May 5 regarding the above named persons.

We did secure the verification of the marriage of Leonard A. Harris and Flossie Louise Bowman. This marriage took place in Catoosa County, Georgia, and is recorded in Book L, page 478 in the Ordinary's Office at Ringgold, Georgia. The marriage took place on 6-25-45 in Rossville, Georgia. We also have verification of the marriage of Arnold L. Griffith and Flossie L. Bowman who were married on 4-22-51 in Rossville, Georgia. We have still been unable to find any verification of the divorce of Miss Bowman from Mr. Harris either in Circuit Court records or Chancery Court records. It would seem that unless Mr. Harris has gotten the divorce from Flossie Bowman that she was still married to him at the time of the birth of the child.

At the time worker talked with Miss Bowman regarding this situation, she did not show any feeling at all about having surrendered her child. She asked no questions about it and did not seem at all concerned about it.

We might suggest that you write to Tracy City, Tennessee, to see if you can get verification of divorce since Mrs. Griffith believes that Leonard Harris now lives around Tracy City. Mrs. Griffith was also certain that she got a divorce from Leonard Harris as she remembers the judge telling her that she could get married again and she insisted that the judge was Judge Kelly. Judge Kelly's circuit includes Tracy City.

We hope this information will be of help to you and if any further information is needed please feel free to call on us.

Very sincerely yours,

APP:
(Miss) Mamie Lou Hall
       County Director

(Miss) Doris June Vinton
       Child Welfare Worker

DJV:ms
cc: Mrs. McGavock

Fig. 24 Vinton Letter (TDPW) 5/13/52

STATE OF TENNESSEE

DEPARTMENT OF PUBLIC WELFARE

STATE OFFICE BUILDING
NASHVILLE 3

. McMAHAN
COMMISSIONER

July 12, 1951

*measure to L a 7/23/51 gm
remailed*

Mr. and Mrs. Walter A. Boehmer
505 So. Sunset Blvd.
Temple City, California

My Dear Mr. and Mrs. Boehmer:

I am glad to be able to inform you that the Board of the
Tennessee Children's Home Society is now reorganized and has met the
requirements for a temporary conditional license which was issued by
this Department on June 30, 1951. When all requirements for the consummation of pending adoptions have been met this license enables the
Tennessee Children's Home Society to give legal consent to the adoption of children already legally received into their guardianship.
It does not authorize the acceptance of new applications to adopt
Tennessee children by residents of other states.

The agreement worked out cooperatively between this Department
and the California Department of Social Welfare in April 1951 was officially approved by the Board of the Tennessee Children's Home Society
on June 28, 1951. According to this agreement both the Tennessee
Children's Home Society and this Department recognizes the California
Department of Social Welfare as the official agency in California to
make the study required by California law relative to the development
and adjustment of the child placed in your home for adoption and the
stability of the adoptive relationship.

Such studies will be made upon referral from this Department.
After the report of the study is received from the California Department of Social Welfare and review is made of all the facts in each
pending adoption the legal consent will be executed by the Tennessee
Children's Home Society and approved by this Department when the adoption is found to be in the best interests of the child. The necessary
legal documents will be forwarded by this Department to the California
Department of Social Welfare. The California Department of Social
Welfare will advise you concerning the filing of the petition for adoption in the California Court and will prepare the necessary report to
the Court in accordance with California law.

Fig. 25 McMahon Letter (TDPW) – Page 1 7/12/51

All communications concerning children whose adoptions have not been legally consummated should be directed to this Department, attention Mrs. Vallie S. Miller, Supervisor of Adoptions.

Any communications concerning children whose adoptions have already been decreed should be directed to Miss Lena Martin, State Superintendent, Tennessee Children's Home Society, 901 Acklen Avenue, Nashville 4, Tennessee.

We regret the long delay in clarifying procedures for you regarding the service you may expect looking toward assistance in settling permanently the status of the child in your home. This has been due to many complexities arising from the disregard of both Tennessee and California laws in the extensive inter-state placement of children by the Shelby County Branch of the Tennessee Children's Home Society which, as you know, is now closed and enjoined by court order from further operations.

We hope your child is progressing satisfactorily under your care. It will take some time yet to clear all the pending adoptions because of the large volume but we wanted you to know that the necessary steps are being taken to insure the legality of adoptions pending with the view of giving security to all the parties concerned.

Very sincerely yours,

J. O. McMahan
Commissioner

JOM/dmc

Fig. 25 McMahon Letter (TDPW)—Page 2 7/12/51

APPLICATION FOR CONFIDENTIAL VERIFICATION OF BIRTH

Copy

Division of Vital Statistics
Department of Public Health
420 Sixth Avenue, North
Nashville 3, Tennessee

Date _July 26, 1951_ 194____

Request certified photostatic copy for purposes of adoption

Verification of the following items is needed for the official purposes of the agency named at the bottom of this form.

Vallie S. Miller

Signature of person making request _Mrs. Vallie S. Miller, Supervisor of Child Welfare_

FILL IN EVERY ITEM IN THIS BOX

1. Full Name of Child _James Arnold Bowman_   2. Cert. No. If Known _2830?_

3. Date of Birth _May_ _8_ _1949_   4. Sex _male_   5. Color _white_
   MONTH   DAY   YEAR

6. Place of Birth: _Jasper_   _Marion_   _Tenn._
   CITY   COUNTY   STATE

7. Full Name of Father _____   8. Maiden Name of Mother _Flossie Louise Bowman_

9. Other Pertinent Data

DO NOT WRITE IN THIS BOX

Corrections of above statements made by vital records office according to facts on file:

DATA ON CERTIFICATE
Consistent with Above Information

Certificate No. _28302 (49)_
File Date _6-8-49_
   This is to verify that the above data as corrected are true and correct according to the record on file in this office. These data are confidential and cannot be used in any manner except for the official purposes of the agency below.

Verified by: _mc_
Date _8-16-57_

Name and address of agency to which verification is to be sent:

Name of Agency _Department of Public Welfare_

Street and No. _Jonas Building_

City and State _Nashville, Tennessee_

RECEIVED

JUL 31 1951

STATE HEALTH DEPT.

Agency's own file number or other identification may be placed below.

Tennessee Dept. of Public Health Form No. 108

Fig. 26 Application For Confidential Verification of Birth 7/26/51

TO THE HONORABLE D. F. BLACKMON, JUDGE OF THE JUVENILE
COURT OF DAVIDSON COUNTY, TENNESSEE

TENNESSEE CHILDREN'S HOME SOCIETY)
            Petitioner

                                        (

)

vs.   No. _____

                                        (

)

LEONARD A. HARRIS and FLOSSIE LOUISE BOWMAN (HARRIS)
                    Defendants   (

Re: JAMES ARNOLD BOWMAN, born May 8, 1949

     Petitioner would respectfully show to the Court:

                             I

     That petitioner is a licensed child-placing agency of the State of
Tennessee, with its principal office and place of business in Nashville,
Davidson County, Tennessee.

                             II

     That defendants, Leonard A. Harris and Flossie Louise Bowman (Harris),
were lawfully married in Rossville, Georgia, on June 25, 1945. That on
the 8th day of May, 1949, in Jasper, Marion County, Tennessee, defendant
Flossie Louise Bowman (Harris) gave birth to a male child, James Arnold
Bowman. The birth certificate of said child, which will be shown to the
Court at the time of the hearing, does not list anyone as the father of
said child in the space provided for same. Petitioner has been unable
to verify any divorce on the part of the defendants. That on the 8th
day of December, 1949, defendant Flossie Louise Bowman (Harris) executed
a certain instrument whereby she purported to surrender said child to
petitioner, and authorized petitioner to keep and care for said child and
to place said child in a suitable home for adoption. Said instrument is

Fig. 27 TCHS v. Harris and Bowman #103-605—Page 1 (date unknown)

support of the child. Petitioner now wishes to complete adoption plans for said child, and in order to carry out these aims, seeks full custody, control and legal guardianship of said child, with the right to act in loco parentis. Petitioner has been unsuccessful in its attempts to locate the defendant. The address of the defendant is unknown and cannot be ascertained upon diligent inquiry.

III

Petitioner therefore avers that said child, James Arnold Bowman, is a dependent, neglected and abandoned child, within the meaning of Sections 10270 and 9572.16 (5) Williams Tennessee Code, and that said child has been wilfully abandoned by its natural parents, the defendants in this action, for more than four consecutive months next preceding institution of this proceeding.

PREMISES CONSIDERED, PETITIONER PRAYS:

1. That service of process by publication be had upon the defendants, Leonard A. Harris and Flossie Louise Bowman (Harris), as required by law, and that they be required to answer, but not under oath, that being expressly waived.

2. That at the hearing of this cause the Honorable Court decree that James Arnold Bowman is a neglected, dependent and abandoned child, he having been wilfully abandoned by his parents, the defendants in this cause, for more than four consecutive months prior to the filing of this petition.

3. That at the hearing of this cause this Honorable Court award the sole and exclusive care, custody and legal guardianship of James Arnold Bowman to petitioner, with the right to place said child in a suitable home for adoption and to act in loco parentis.

4. That petitioner have such other, further and general relief as the justice of the cause may require.

Fig. 27 TCHS v. Harris and Bowman—Page 2

for said child, and in order to carry out these aims, seeks full custody control and legal guardianship of said child, with the right to act in loco parentis. Petitioner has been unsuccessful in its attempts to loca the defendant. The address of the defendant is unknown and cannot be as certained upon diligent inquiry.

III

Petitioner therefore avers that said child, James Arnold Bowman, is a dependent, neglected and abandoned child, within the meaning of Sectio 10270 and 9572.16 (5) Williams Tennessee Code, and that said child has been wilfully abandoned by its natural parents, the defendants in this action, for more than four consecutive months next preceding institution of this proceeding.

PREMISES CONSIDERED, PETITIONER PRAYS:

1. That service of process by publication be had upon the defendan Leonard A. Harris and Flossie Louise Bowman (Harris), as required by law and that they be required to answer, but not under oath, that being expressly waived.

2. That at the hearing of this cause the Honorable Court decree th James Arnold Bowman is a neglected, dependent and abandoned child, he having been wilfully abandoned by his parents, the defendants in this cause, for more than four consecutive months prior to the filing of this petition.

3. That at the hearing of this cause this Honorable Court award the sole and exclusive care, custody and legal guardianship of James Arnold Bowman to petitioner, with the right to place said child in a suitable home for adoption and to act in loco parentis.

4. That petitioner have such other, further and general relief as the justice of the cause may require.

TENNESSEE CHILDREN'S HOME SOCIETY

W. Raymond Denney, Pres. Board of Directo

(Miss) Lena Martin, State Superintendent

Attorney for Petitioner

Fig. 27 TCHS v. HARRIS AND BOWMAN – Page 3

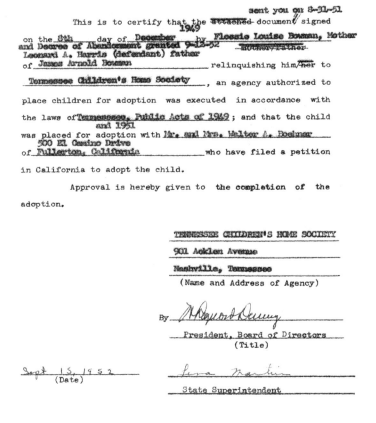

State of California   Department of Social Welfare

CERTIFICATION OF RELINQUISHMENT

                                        sent you on 8-31-51
            This is to certify that the attached document signed
                             1949
on the 8th day of December by Flossie Louise Bowman, Mother
and Decree of Abandonment granted 9-12-52   Mother, Father.
Leonard A. Harris (defendant) father
of James Arnold Bowman   relinquishing him/her to

Tennessee Children's Home Society , an agency authorized to

place children for adoption was executed in accordance with

the laws of Tennessee, Public Acts of 1949 ; and that the child
                   and 1951
was placed for adoption with Mr. and Mrs. Walter A. Boehner
          500 El Camino Drive
of Fullerton, California   who have filed a petition

in California to adopt the child.

            Approval is hereby given to the completion of the

adoption.

                     TENNESSEE CHILDREN'S HOME SOCIETY

                     901 Acklen Avenue

                     Nashville, Tennessee
                     (Name and Address of Agency)

                  By _____

                     President, Board of Directors
                              (Title)

    Sept 15, 1952   _____
        (Date)
                          State Superintendent

Form Adop M75, Revised January 1952

Fig. 28 TCHS Certificate of Relinquishment 9/15/52

FILED
MAR 4 - 1953
B. E. SMITH
COUNTY CLERK

IN THE SUPERIOR COURT OF THE STATE OF CALIFORNIA

IN AND FOR THE COUNTY OF ORANGE

IN THE MATTER OF THE ADOPTION)	No. A-22307
OF)	DECREE OF ADOPTION
JAMES ARNOLD BOWMAN, a Minor)	

HOOPER AND MILLER
ATTORNEYS AT LAW
SUITE 1102 WM. FOX BLDG.
608 SOUTH HILL ST.
LOS ANGELES 14
VANDIKE 1061

WALTER A. BOEHNER and SIDONIA C. BOEHNER, having presented their petition praying for approval of their adoption of
the above named minor child, and the said matter coming on regu-
larly to be heard, GEORGE A. HOOPER appearing as attorney for
the petitioners, and there appearing before the Court the petitioners and the above named minor child who were examined by
the Court, each separately, from which examination it is found
that the petitioners are husband and wife, and are residents of
the County of Orange, State of California.

That on the 5th day of May, 1949, the above named chi
was born in the City of Jasper, County of Marion, State of Tenn
see, unto FLOSSIE LOUISE BOWMAN HARRIS, wife of LEONARD A. HARR

That heretofore a Court of competent jurisdiction in
the State of Tennessee declared said child free from the custod
of said parents and deprived said parents of the custody of sai
child; that the TENNESSEE CHILDREN'S HOME SOCIETY, an incorpora

Fig. 29 Decree of Adoption (CA) 3/4/53

February 16, 1953

Mr. Ralph L. Goff, Area Director
Department of Social Welfare
1.5 South Spring Street
Los Angeles 12, California

Attention: Mrs. Helen Chandler, Adoptions Worker

Re: Adoption of James Arnold Bowman by
Mr. and Mrs. Walter L. Boehner

Dear Mr. Goff:

We are making a monthly review of the adoptions still pending
of children in the guardianship of the Tennessee Children's Home
Society and find that on October 2n, 1952 we transmitted to your
office the necessary documents for the consummation of the above
adoption.

We realize that this case may not yet have been heard by the
Court but would appreciate a report from you concerning its status
and, if the final decree has been granted, we would appreciate your
communicating with the attorney relative to providing us with a
certified copy of the decree and forwarding the documents necessary
for securing a new birth certificate.

We appreciate your cooperation in bringing this matter to a
satisfactory conclusion.

Yours very truly,

(Mrs.) Christine C. Reynolds
Commissioner

CCR/dmc

cc: Miss Bessie C. Irvin

Fig. 30 Reynolds Letter (TDPW) 2/16/53

Earl Warren
Governor

STATE OF CALIFORNIA

Department of Social Welfare

CHARLES I. SCHOTTLAND
DIRECTOR
Los Angeles
March 20, 1953

MAR 27 1953

Mrs. Christine C. Reynolds, Commissioner
Department of Public Welfare
State Office Building
Nashville, Tennessee

ADDRESS REPLY TO:

145 South Spring Street
Los Angeles 12

Dear Mrs. Reynolds:

                    Adoption of James Arnold Bowman
                    By Mr. and Mrs. Walter L. Boehner
                    Or 1348 Ad

        We are enclosing a certified copy of the order of adoption granted
by the Superior Court of the State of California, in and for the County
of Orange, in the above-captioned matter. This order was granted on March
4, 1953. The attorney for Mr. and Mrs. Boehner, Mr. George A. Hooper,
is taking responsibility for sending the documents for the issuance of
a new birth certificate.

        Our department is now closing its file and considers this matter
completed.

                                        Very truly yours,

                                        Mrs. Helen Chandler
                                        Adoptions Worker

Attachment

Fig. 31 Chandler Letter (CDSW) 3/20/53

EPILOGUE

On February 24, 2014, I received my latest book find entitled, "*No Momma, I didn't DIE*", by Devereaux R. Bruch, born Nell Howell, on her experiences as a victim of Georgia Tann and life as an Adoptee from the late 1930's. What struck me was an entry on pages 111-112 where Ms. Howell cites the discovery of a mass grave in the back of Tann's orphanage home on Poplar in Memphis. I had not read up to this time, this information of the remains of 40 infants found there. After living this story for five years, I was neither shocked nor surprised that the infamous Tann would do such a despicable deed. What about the 200-400 children who died under Tann's care, just in a 4-month period in the early 1940's? Where did they go and who speaks for them? Ironically, on the same day, I received my latest search request and order back from the Orange County Superior Court; no record found of my California adoption case allegedly completed March 4, 1953, by Order of the Court. Case documents were forged in-office by the Hooper and Miller law office in Los Angeles, disseminated as proper filings to DSS in Sacramento and to the TCHS, and the California portion of the adoption was finalized. What is left now in my investigative attempts is a reply from the Davidson County Juvenile Court, 100 Woodland, Nashville, TN 37213. On February 21, 2014, I sent off a written request for search and copies of the juvenile court file #103-605 which contains my abandonment and neglect hearing, Proof of Service by Publication and supporting case documents. We'll see if they find the case cited, and, if all the pertinent documents are present.

On February 21, 2014, I mailed the submission requirements of this book to Sterling Publishing of New York; I hope they find it acceptable. I wrote this book for two reasons, one, to document my history and family roots to our children; and, two, as an investigative record and resource to be used to cause the revocation of my unlawful adoption and restoration of my birth name through civil lawsuit. I have been met with denial and rejection from all state agencies involved in my adoption. The only reason I received copies of my adoption files from the Tennessee Department of Children's Services was due to a law ordering them to do so. When I specifically asked the agency to conduct an investigation into my findings, their reply was "Good Luck" with that. Upon personal telephone contact with Department of Social Services in Sacramento in January 2014, the department declined any assistance and referred me to the Orange County Superior Court; and we now know how that turned out. So like a kid with a dominos set, knocking the possible leads down one at a time; sooner or later they all fall.

CPSIA information can be obtained
at www.ICGtesting.com
Printed in the USA
BVOW09s1131260917
495935BV00001B/11/P

9 781493 187041